D1593852

Praise for *The Leader's Compass for Law Enforcement Professionals*

"*The Leader's Compass for Law Enforcement Professionals* is a personal journey of discovery and leadership for police leaders confronting the everyday challenges of leading in a police organization. Roy E. Alston, PhD, author of *RadioActive Leadership* and *Tarnished Honor*, and Dennis F. Haley of Academy Leadership really bring the challenges of police supervision alive in a clear and easy-to-follow parable for anyone aspiring to be a better police supervisor and leader.

"I am not a big fan of leadership books, because they fail to address the context of police leadership challenges. This is not the case regarding *The Leader's Compass for Law Enforcement Professionals*. Roy E. Alston and Dennis Haley have shined a bright light on the challenges specific to police supervision and police leadership and have offered a great solution—creating a personal leadership philosophy. I recommend this book to anyone who aspires to lead in a police organization."

—Michael P. Downing, Deputy Chief, Commanding Officer, Counter-Terrorism and Special Operations Bureau, Los Angeles Police Department

"Police organizations, like any other organization, deserve excellent leadership. If police organizations are going to be great, then police leadership has to be great. *The Leader's Compass for*

Law Enforcement Professionals serves as a guide to help police leaders become great and therefore help police organizations to be great. This book and the adaptation of solid leadership philosophies to policing are long overdue. A great book! Every police supervisor and police leader should be issued a copy of *The Leader's Compass for Law Enforcement Professionals* and required to read it with the end goal of creating and publishing a personal leadership philosophy."

—Malik Aziz, Deputy Chief, Homeland Security/Special Operations Division, Dallas Police Department

"*The Leader's Compass for Law Enforcement Professionals* is definitely not a 'flavor of the month' leadership book written by some academic who has not experienced what it is like to be a police officer and to lead in a police organization. I recommend this book for anyone aspiring to be a police leader and for those who are already in a police leadership role."

—Jose G. Munoz, Detective, Dallas County Hospital District Police Department

BOOKS FROM ACADEMY LEADERSHIP PUBLISHING

The Leader's Compass for Law Enforcement Professionals: A Values-Based Approach to Influencing People, Accomplishing Goals, and Improving Your Organization

The Accountability Compass: Moving from "The Blame Game" to Collaboration

The Core Values Compass: Moving from Cynicism to a Core Values Culture

The Corporate Compass: Providing Focus and Alignment to Stay the Course, 2nd Edition

My Father's Compass: Leadership Lessons for an Immigrant Son

The Leader's Compass: A Personal Leadership Philosophy Is Your Key to Success, 2nd Edition

Inspiring Leadership: Character and Ethics Matter

"Leadership is the art of getting someone else to do something you want done because he wants to do it."

— Gen. Dwight D. Eisenhower

THE LEADER'S COMPASS FOR
LAW ENFORCEMENT PROFESSIONALS

A Values-Based Approach to Influencing People, Accomplishing Goals, and Improving Your Organization

ROY E. ALSTON, PhD
DENNIS F. HALEY

ISBN: 978-0-9727323-7-6

Library of Congress Control Number: 2012955165

Academy Leadership books are available at special quantity discounts to use as premiums and sales promotions, or for use in corporate training programs. For more information, please call Academy Leadership at 610-783-0630, or write to: 10120 Valley Forge Circle, King of Prussia, PA 19406.

Printed in the United States of America.

All law enforcement agencies have mission statements and organizational principles that guide their officers and focus their activities. Most law enforcement leaders recognize that developing these clearly articulated statements is time well spent; they help keep the agency or department on track and pointed toward clear goals. A written personal leadership philosophy, which we call the "leader's compass," achieves the same purpose on an individual level; it lets people know what you value, how you will act, and how you will measure performance, with the additional benefits of making the workplace less stressful and more productive. And, like a compass, it helps to keep you, the leader, on course.

Table of Contents

Acknowledgments i

Introduction iii

The Command Leadership Philosophy xiii

Part One

Chapter 1—Welcome to Sector Three 1

Chapter 2—First Assignment: Impossible? 9

Chapter 3—Convention Clean Up 17

Chapter 4—First Shift 21

Chapter 5—Neighborly Advice 41

Part Two

Chapter 6—The Breakfast Club Meets Again 53

Chapter 7—Notes, Napkins, and New Ideas 59

Chapter 8—More Lessons in Leadership 65

Chapter 9—A Heart-to-Heart with Hardy 75

Chapter 10—Answers and an Assignment 81

Chapter 11—Jenkins's Warning 89

Part Three

Chapter 12—Best and Worst 95

Chapter 13—The Rifle 105

Chapter 14—Marriage Counseling 111

Chapter 15—Right and Wrong 117

Chapter 16—Clear and Concise. 127

Chapter 17—Narcotics and Vice 135

Chapter 18—Blind Spots 147

Chapter 19—The Breakfast Club Reconvenes 155

Part Four

Chapter 20—Honest Assessments 161

Chapter 21—Stanley's Policy 171

Chapter 22—The Marker 179

Chapter 23—The Nail That Sticks Up 183

Epilogue—Validation 191

My Leadership Philosophy: Adam McGraw 203

Your Leader's Compass 207

My Leadership Philosophy: Roy E. Alston, PhD 215

My Leadership Philosophy: Catrina Shead 219

My Leadership Philosophy: Vernon Hale 223

Addendum: More Thoughts on Leadership 227

Academy Leadership Services 251

Books from Academy Leadership Publishing 261

ACKNOWLEDGMENTS

Many people made possible the publication of this book, especially the staff of Academy Leadership who developed and presented *The Leader's Compass* in numerous seminars. Their experience in coaching thousands of clients in writing personal leadership philosophies gave us the material from which to build this resource for all aspiring leaders.

Thanks to Captain H.J. Halliday, United States Navy (Retired), former skipper of the USS *Nevada*, whose command leadership philosophy is the basis for the one developed by the main character in the book.

Thanks also to the many men and women of the U.S. Navy, the U.S. Army, and the U.S. law enforcement community, who, over the years, have taken the time to teach the authors about leadership. Thanks to the many commanders, police officers, professors, cadets, midshipmen, spouses, and children who have been a part of our individual learning experiences.

Special thanks go to class members of the May 2012 Sergeant Supervisory Series at the Caruth Police Institute at Dallas, who provided invaluable input and feedback on the project.

INTRODUCTION

By Mark Stainbrook, Assistant Chief,
San Diego Harbor Police Department

LAPD Sergeant George Khoury was the best supervisor I ever worked for. He was one of those humble leaders you wanted to follow because he led by example. You respected George because he knew his job, but he also always had time to listen to what you had to say. Above all things, George loved making good arrests. It was his excitement and enthusiasm that motivated our unit to go out every night and "hook and book" more bad guys.

Back in the late 1990s, I was George's assistant squad leader in an anti-gang unit nicknamed CRASH. It was a tough time for cops in the LAPD. The infamous Rampart corruption scandal had driven down morale across the department. Everyone in our CRASH unit knew a few cops who were absolutely miserable at the time, but our unit was largely unaffected. Why? As I learned from George, it is the first-line supervisor who always bears the largest responsibility for individual and unit morale—regardless of the circumstances.

In every sense of the word, George took *care* of his people. He made sure we received commendations, got the flex-hours and days off we needed, and that our equipment and training were up-to-date. George knew that cops love good weapons, new gear, and intense training. He set the right conditions to help us do our job, and we responded by staying focused on the mission.

George also proved to be an excellent judge of people. He knew how to mix partners with complementary skills and temperaments. He trained the right people for the right positions in order to get the best out of them. Training was frequent, and we became a tighter unit because of it. All the members of CRASH understood their roles, and George made you comfortable with yours. George made each one of us feel important to the overall success of the unit.

I thought of George as I read this book about a young police sergeant facing difficult leadership challenges from supervisors, peers, and subordinates. This book asks the question: "How can first-line supervisors maintain integrity and grow as a leader with so many competing demands on their time, attention, and loyalty?" The authors, Roy Alston and Dennis Haley, provide an excellent roadmap for new police leaders and recommend a process that enables you, the reader, to develop your "personal leadership philosophy." Your "PLP" is a brief document that helps you define what is most important to you personally as a leader and serves as your "leader's compass," as mentioned in the title of this book. When you distribute your PLP to those who count on you for leadership, it becomes a tool for communicating your expectations, as well as what you absolutely will not tolerate.

I wholeheartedly recommend that you write a PLP, which I believe you will find challenging, but also very rewarding. It is not easy to explore your own leadership strengths and weaknesses. Like Sgt. Adam McGraw in this story, I have my own written PLP, which I have shared with my staff in several capacities over two decades of law enforcement leadership. It is a document that was years in the making, and it is still continually evolving. I call my PLP "Leadership in the Trenches," because it was born from leading people face-to-face on the front lines—on the streets of L.A. and in the desert of Iraq.

In 2003, I was deployed to Iraq as a Marine Corps Major. While I was there, everything that I had ever learned about leadership was put to the test. I saw some leaders exercise basic leadership principles in courageous ways, under tremendous pressure. I saw other leaders either ignore or fail to lead by those very same principles, often at the expense of their people.

When I returned to the LAPD following my deployment, I was a relatively new sergeant in need of focus and direction, so I set about writing my first PLP. Working from what I had learned in Iraq and years in the military, I tried as best as I could to apply my military lessons to the task of leading cops in a big city. The first draft of the PLP was little more than a set of bullet points, but those bullets helped me organize my thoughts. Then I fleshed them out in the form of stories and examples.

In a nutshell, my PLP begins with leading myself:

- Be on time
- Be in the right uniform
- Be ready to work
- Be ready, so you don't have to get ready; and
- Take care of those you lead, not just physically, but mentally and emotionally

Thanks to my PLP, everyone I work with knows that these are the standards I set for myself, and that I expect no less from them. My PLP is plainly written in black and white, but it is not set in stone. PLPs are living documents. Since your PLP is based on your personal reflections, it should be tweaked periodically to reflect your new insights, experiences, roles, and responsibilities. In this way, your PLP can offer an avenue for meaningful discussions about leadership with your comrades on the force. Show them your latest version and ask what they think. How do they feel when they read it? Ask them which parts communicate to them and which parts don't. Brilliant insights can come out of these talks—insights about leadership and about yourself.

Your PLP can help you deal with what I think is the single most grievous mistake commonly made by law enforcement leaders: the reluctance to confront officers about poor choices and bad behavior. First-line supervisors are often the only leaders with enough close daily contact to recognize the signs that a fellow cop is either troubled or getting into trouble. Yet too many police supervisors choose to look the other way. For young supervisors, perhaps this is understandable due to a lack of proper training. But I also see very senior supervisors who have lost their inner fire and refuse to deal with serious issues among their subordinates. Their entire organization suffers as a result.

Most of the personnel issues that I deal with on a daily basis involve complaints that employees make against each other. I find it interesting that the same cops, who, without hesitation, will race to any call for assistance from a brother or sister officer, will also figuratively kill each other with workplace rumors, thoughtless gossip, and malicious, undermining behavior. I often wonder whether this self-destructive culture helps explain the high rates of divorce, alcoholism, and suicide among police officers. Sustaining a positive and respectful workplace atmosphere is one of the most important roles of a law enforcement leader. You'll find that your PLP is an invaluable tool for this purpose. Once you define in clear language what you will and will not tolerate, you can establish a working environment in which mutual respect prevails, and officers won't fear asking for help when they experience personal difficulties.

This story of Sgt. Adam McGraw, as he develops his personal leadership philosophy, also offers an illustration of how to use the PLP to deal with a range of serious first-line leadership issues. For instance, I think the hardest leadership position to hold is that of a newly promoted first-line supervisor who must now lead their former peers. This leader is often placed in charge of personal friends or former coworkers, some of whom may have more training and more time on the job. Under such circumstances, police officers love to give their "rookie" supervisors a hard time, just to see what they can get away with. All of your weaknesses, faults, and past mistakes are instantly shared with everyone. Some will try to use this knowledge to undermine your authority.

Writing out your PLP as a first-time, first-line supervisor can help you in two ways. First, identifying what you believe in will help you stay strong mentally and maintain the willpower to overcome both passive and aggressive challenges to your leadership. It will help you define what you stand for as the leader and what your team needs to know to be successful. Distributing your PLP is an effective and straightforward way to communicate these expectations to your subordinates. Although many officers will already be meeting your expectations when you issue your PLP, you can prevent bad behavior from problem officers by taking a firm position from the start. For example, if you know that one or two officers on your watch are known for making inappropriate remarks in front of female officers, your PLP can make it clear that you demand a professional work environment and that you will not tolerate any form of sexual harassment.

You will get tested. When you do, your PLP challenges you to "walk your talk" and take the appropriate action. Failure in this respect guarantees that you will quickly lose all credibility. You will make some mistakes. You will not always be able to live up to the letter of your PLP. Consistency and accountability are hard to maintain, especially over a long period of time. An old cliché about good leadership applies here: It is a marathon, not a sprint. Come back to your PLP to stay on track.

Because leadership can be lonely and frustrating at times, I always recommend that leaders find a "Like-Minded Leader," or an LML, as I call them. Adam McGraw finds one in this story, and you will see the value he finds in being able to talk confidentially with someone who knows exactly what he's going through. Keep in mind that no one leads alone. I have seen some good leaders fail by trying to do everything by themselves. Regardless of your dedication, you can't be on the job 24/7. Your success relies on building a leadership team with those around you. Whenever you see a successful leader, you usually see that leader surrounded by other successful leaders. It's not a happy coincidence. Those leaders have found their LMLs.

Finally, you will see in this story how Adam McGraw would be lost without his mentor. When I find leaders who impress me, I ask them very directly to mentor me and be a personal resource for me. There is nothing better than using the knowledge from other police leaders in this way. Books, videos, and other leadership resources can be very helpful, but the book you are holding right now will create the most value for you if it inspires you to seek out a flesh-and-blood mentor. I make sure I take my mentors out for coffee once in a while, just so I can pick their brains about the latest leadership issues I'm facing. It is amazing how much wisdom a $3 cup of coffee buys!

I don't think George Khoury ever wrote out his PLP. He certainly had a philosophy, and we all sensed what it was, but it raises the question of whether you can be an excellent leader like George without a PLP. I suppose you can, but I personally wouldn't want to try. We can't all be George Khoury, after all. He had a sixth sense about how to stay the course as a leader. The rest of us, I think, could use a compass.

Times have changed, too, since I was George's assistant in the early 1990s. We have flash mobs now. Citizens make videos of arrests and put them on YouTube. Online police message boards are filled with anonymous invective posted by police officers about their fellow officers. Leadership is challenged every day in ways that would have been unimaginable ten or twenty years ago.

The changing times have also brought new opportunities, but we will all need to make adjustments if we want to make the most of them. The police officers now joining the force are smarter, better educated, and more experienced than those of any previous generation. The conflicts in Iraq and Afghanistan have produced thousands of military veterans who join our ranks with combat experience and excellent training courtesy of the most highly advanced war machine in history.

The challenge for law enforcement leadership in the coming years could not be clearer. How do we fully leverage the skills and sophistication of these new young officers without causing conflict with those of higher rank who may have less experience and technical capabilities? Greater and greater trust must be placed with subordinate leaders, who are becoming ever more specialized in their areas of expertise. We need to push leadership responsibility down through the organization and allow junior police officers to take more ownership of projects and programs.

For example, I have a few junior officers in my department who are much more technically savvy than just about anyone at the command staff levels. Egos need to be checked at the door if such a circumstance is to work. I understand that I need to accept that I cannot be an expert on everything. There is far too much information to learn, read, and review. So I must trust my junior officers. Without trust, there is no leadership.

This simple fact underlines another frank conversation that we need to be having within law enforcement. If our core mission is to reduce crime and increase public safety, police leaders must become proficient at using crime statistics and other data to measure productivity and deploy resources. Budget cuts have severely impacted government services in recent years, and employee pay, benefits, and pensions will continue to be attacked in such a fiscal environment. If law enforcement is to remain valuable and relevant, we need to rely on statistical performance measures to showcase what we do and protect our image. But all this starts with the officers on the street. If we fail on that front, if we fail to provide outstanding first-line leadership, we all will fail. Period.

In the final analysis, leadership all comes down to helping people. I have never met anyone who wants to be led by someone who doesn't care. By the same token, I don't think there is a greater satisfaction in the world than giving of yourself to help others. Whenever I get tired, frustrated, and irritable (an inevitable price, I believe, of doing leadership right), I recharge myself with the memories of the many wonderful comrades I have had the privilege to lead, and to follow. Your PLP gives you the opportunity to make use of your own memories, of the best and worst you have experienced in leadership, and transform them into principles for action and a roadmap to an exciting and fulfilling career.

THE COMMAND LEADERSHIP PHILOSOPHY

In the 1980s, the United States Navy conducted a study to determine why some ships performed well consistently in every measure of effectiveness, from inspections to combat drills, whereas others were consistently average in performance. The answer was deceptively simple: It all started with the skipper. The results did not surprise experienced Navy men and women; a sailor can tell a lot about the command climate on a ship simply by going aboard, looking around at maintenance, cleanliness, and seaworthiness, and talking to the crew to determine their spirit and attitude. The pivotal role played by the commander is underscored by this dictum, which is gospel throughout all the nation's armed forces: The commander is responsible for everything the unit does or fails to do.

Talk about your straightforward guidelines.

Leadership plays the central role in what military units can accomplish. The same is true in police organizations. This is why a good boss—a good leader—is responsible and is out in front of the organization.

Because leadership begins with the boss—with the commander, in military terms—both the U.S. Army and the U.S. Navy require new commanders to write a leadership philosophy, a written document that lets subordinates know: This is where I stand, and this is what I want. This explicit statement of standards and expectations provides general guidance on what to do and how to do it. In addition, if the boss's actions are consistent with his or her stated beliefs, subordinates learn to trust the leader. A boss who says one thing and does another, or states one set of values and lives by another, may get people to follow during easy times, but when things get tough, people want leaders of character.

What follows is a fictional account of how one police leader developed his leader's compass.

PART ONE

CHAPTER 1

Welcome to Sector Three

Sgt. Adam McGraw steered his car down Juniper Street and turned right into the dim parking lot behind the Midtown East police substation. For the first time in his career, he pulled into a row of spaces along a brick wall marked "SUPERVISORS ONLY."

The previous morning, McGraw had been promoted—along with dozens of other members of the Central City Police Department—in a solemn ceremony at the nearby convention center. After eight years as a patrol officer, McGraw was now a sergeant. *And not just any sergeant, either,* he reminded himself as he gathered his things from the passenger seat and opened the door. *I've been assigned to the overnight shift in the toughest police district in the city.*

"Hey, Quickdraw!" a voice called out in the darkness as McGraw locked his car. He didn't have to look up to know that the voice belonged to Fred Hitchcock, a veteran patrolman McGraw had worked with several years ago in the Northeast district. With a mental sigh, McGraw looked in Hitchcock's direction, but he didn't smile. He had never liked the nickname Hitchcock had given him.

"*Sergeant* McGraw," Hitchcock pronounced slowly as he approached, his raised eyebrows illuminated by streetlights. "Congratulations on the promotion. I guess that's the last time I'll be calling you 'Quickdraw McGraw.'"

"You guessed right, Hitch," McGraw replied in a purposefully light tone as he shoved his keys into his pocket. The two men started walking toward the back door of the substation. "How are you doing?"

"I'm in this rathole, so what does that tell you?" Hitch responded with a laugh. "I mean, working first watch in this district is a great place to break in a new sergeant like you. But for me? With twelve years on the streets?" This time, Hitch's laugh was unmistakably bitter. "Somebody in HQ hates me."

"When did they send you here?" McGraw asked the other man, eyeing Hitch warily. He knew that wherever Hitch went, trouble had a way of following.

"Eleven months ago," Hitch replied as they neared the building. "I was still up in the Northeast district when I got written up on a few chicken-crap violations. They sent me here, and that opened up a spot for a rookie in the Northeast. I think that kid must know someone in HQ."

McGraw swung open the rusted door to the substation, grateful for a reason not to answer. The hallway in front of him was dimly lit by flickering fluorescent bulbs. McGraw took a deep breath as he stepped inside and immediately jerked his head back in reaction to a strong odor.

"That smell is the lockup, to the left," Hitch explained, smiling at McGraw's grimace. "You know which sector you're heading?"

Midtown East was split up into four patrol sectors. On each shift, a patrol sector was headed by a sergeant who supervised a team of eight to twelve patrol officers to cover each beat.

"They told me Patrol Sector Three," McGraw answered, feeling his stomach clench for a moment as he wondered—not for the first time—what the position held in store for him.

"That's mine, too," Hitch exclaimed. "We'll be working together again!"

McGraw hoped that the coincidence would turn out to be a good one. "Which part of the division is that?"

"The worst part," Hitch responded without hesitation, taking the lead as the two men rounded a corner in the hallway. "Sector Three has some office buildings, a few hotels, and the convention center on the near side."

Hitch slowed, then stopped walking altogether. A conspiratorial gleam appeared in his eyes, and he motioned for McGraw to stop as well. "That's all fine in the daytime, but at night the vagrants, homeless, and graffiti artists take over—you'll see. Then, on the other side of the convention center, there's the Walnut and Grant Streets area, with the bars, the nightclubs, the drug dealing, and the hookers." Hitch rolled his eyes. "Most nights that corner is a real drunk and disorderly carnival. Go a few more blocks further out, and we got Pleasantville, which is never dull."

"*Un*-Pleasantville?" McGraw used the cops' nickname for the high-crime neighborhood. "That's in Sector Three?" *Great.*

"I think they planned it this way," Hitchcock confirmed. He lowered his voice as he presented what was clearly his pet theory. "They put all the garbage everyone hates into one single sector. Then they take everyone they don't like and they bury them in that sector, on first watch."

"Is that right?" McGraw wasn't thrilled to be working with Hitch again, but he knew Hitch was often a source of useful information. Hopefully, Hitch's last revelation wouldn't turn out to be true.

"Right or wrong, that's the way it is," Hitchcock replied with a shrug. "Every cop assigned to first watch in Three has either messed something up or ticked someone off. Remember that children's show, about the Land of Misfit Toys? That's us here in Three. We're stuck in Screw-up City, and you're our new mayor."

Hitch laughed at his own cleverness. McGraw didn't join him. "You're not trying to scare me, are you, Hitch?" McGraw asked as he started walking again.

Hitch shook his head. "I just want you to be ready."

"Don't worry about that," replied McGraw. "I've been getting ready for a long time."

It was true. McGraw had been tempted to take the sergeant's test as soon as he was eligible, during his fourth year as a patrol officer. But he'd ultimately decided to wait and finish college instead. He spent three more years taking night classes and online courses, and had finally been awarded his bachelor's degree in criminal justice two years ago. Then, right after graduation, he started studying for the sergeant's test, even taking special prep classes offered by the police association. He was pleased when he tested near the top of the class on the sergeant's exam and remained at the top after the assessment center. All his studying and practice had paid off.

A nudge from Hitch snapped McGraw out of his reverie. "There's Gus, the shift lieutenant," Hitch said, jerking his head toward a man who was walking toward them. "I'll see ya later."

Lt. Jack Gustafson was a tall, thin man with a heavy brow and a lantern jaw. "You McGraw?" he asked, without extending his hand. "Come with me."

They walked over to the main meeting room, where detail would be called soon. Gus looked McGraw up and down before speaking. "You and Hitchcock—are you two buddies?"

"I know him," McGraw replied evenly. "We were both in Northeast for a few years."

"I hope you're not buddies," Gus said with a scowl. "Because, I gotta tell you, Hitchcock is the worst kind of cop. He's highly motivated and prone to poor judgment, which is a lethal combination. Guys like him always go down eventually. Sometimes they take their sergeants with them." Gus fixed McGraw with a pointed look. "Got it?"

"I got it."

"Good." Gus cleared his throat, then sat down at his desk and shuffled through some papers. He spoke without looking at McGraw. "You've got ten officers in your sector on this shift. You'll want to put Williams—the woman over there—on parking tickets, because that's about all she's good for. Ramsey and Somers should take the patrol wagon because they're big and tough. Prisoners are scared of them. The other seven are on patrol, which is not a lot, so you need to be out there, too."

Finally, Gus looked up at McGraw. "I don't want a house mouse for my first shift sergeant in Three."

"I like patrol," McGraw said. He was trying to be agreeable, although in his opinion, Gus wasn't making it easy.

"Like it or not, I want you out there on the streets, okay?" Gus reiterated as he shifted a sheaf of papers to the other side of the desk. He paused for a moment, then continued. "Now the other troublemaker I should warn you about is Hardy."

Gus gestured toward a trim, athletic-looking patrol officer standing alone by the wall on the far side of the room. "Hardy was kicked back to patrol from plainclothes Narcotics," Gus explained. "I don't know what he did wrong, but I assume it had something to do with his mouth and his attitude. He's got a chip on his shoulder and someone higher up doesn't like him, so steer clear of him."

Just then, the substation chief walked in, accompanied by a burly grey-haired man fully turned out in a dark, double-breasted tuxedo. "There's Chief Robinson with our guest tonight,"

Gus murmured as his eyes followed the new arrivals across the room. "You recognize him?"

McGraw shook his head.

"That's Herman Duncan, the big real estate guy. He's got a lot of juice with the Chamber of Commerce, too." In the flickering fluorescent light, surrounded by dirty, scuffed walls covered in peeling paint, Duncan's formalwear and perfectly cut hair looked strangely out of place. "He must have come straight from a charity event," Gus speculated.

"What's he doing here?" McGraw asked, genuinely curious.

"I'll introduce you once he's done talking," Gus replied, turning his attention back to the piles of paper on his desk. "He's got some concerns about your sector."

First Assignment: Impossible?

"Can I have your attention, everyone?" the chief called out, sweeping his eyes over the room. "Let's get everyone settled down here."

About fifty patrol officers were assembled in the substation's main room, seated on benches and pale blue plastic chairs.

"Our guest tonight," Chief Robinson continued once the dull roar had subsided, "is someone many of you already know. Herman Duncan owns Duncan Development, and he's also head of the Chamber of Commerce committee on conventions and tourism, which is why he's here tonight." The chief motioned toward the man in the tuxedo, who inclined his head. "Mr. Duncan has stopped by after the Heart Foundation Ball to fill us in about a special event coming up at the convention center."

With that, Chief Robinson stepped back and nodded to Duncan, who moved to a spot directly in front of the seated group. McGraw, who was seated near the back of the room, leaned slightly forward.

"Thanks, Chief," Duncan began. "First and foremost, I want to thank you and everybody here for your service to the city." Duncan had a magnetic smile and a grand way of speaking. "In four weeks, we've got an event coming to the city that's really going to put this police district to the test. The convention center will be hosting the annual meeting of the American Travel Industry Association."

Duncan paused, then began to walk slowly across the front of the meeting room as he continued to speak. "Now, why is that so special? Well, because it means two thousand of the most important people in the travel industry will be right here in town, right in this neighborhood. These are the people who tell everyone else in the country where to spend their travel dollars."

Duncan turned and began to pace in the other direction, making brief eye contact with various police officers as he did so. "To put it in plain English, having them here, walking our streets day and night, puts our city's national image on the line. When their convention ends and they all fly home, we want them to be telling everyone they know what a great town Central City is. We want them all to recommend Central City as a top-notch tourist destination."

McGraw felt his jaw tighten. He, like everyone else in the room, knew what Duncan was getting at. For this convention to be a winner for the city, all the panhandlers, homeless, hookers, drunks, and drug dealers in Midtown East would need to disappear for a week.

"Most of the travel industry conventioneers will be staying in hotels right here in Midtown East," Duncan continued, spreading his hands as though to indicate the city around them. "At the Chamber of Commerce, we want to be able to assure our guests that they will feel comfortable strolling the streets at all hours."

He held up a finger and tapped his chest. "Personally, I want to feel confident that they will all be safe from harm. So I'll be talking to the chief in the coming weeks about how all of us can work together to clean up the neighborhood. We want to make sure this convention is a great opportunity to show the rest of the country what a special place Central City is."

Finished, Duncan beamed what McGraw suspected was a practiced smile around the room. Then he turned to thank the chief, who dismissed the group.

As the assembly broke up, McGraw continued to watch Duncan, who approached Gus and shook his hand. Soon, the two men were engaged in what looked like a serious conversation. McGraw was just beginning to wonder if the lieutenant had forgotten about him when Gus waved McGraw over and introduced him to Duncan.

As they shook hands, Duncan looked at McGraw with the intense stare of a man accustomed to getting his way. "Sergeant, I was just telling Gus that while walking over here from the Windsor Hotel, I must have seen a half-dozen homeless men. I was approached twice by panhandlers, and once by some low-life who asked if I wanted to buy 'weed.'" Duncan pursed his lips.

"I'm sorry to hear that sir," McGraw said. *And I think I know where you're going with this conversation, too.*

"I told the guy, 'Do I look like someone who wants to buy weed?'" Duncan continued. "And do you know what he said? He said, 'Well, why else would you be in this neighborhood this late?'" Duncan raised his eyebrows. "Apparently the street people assume that your patrol sector becomes an open-air marijuana market each night after 10:00."

I was right, McGraw confirmed, though he didn't feel any satisfaction at the thought.

Gus interjected, "This is McGraw's first night assigned to this division, Mr. Duncan. But he's a quick study. He was top of his class in the sergeant's exam and just completed seven weeks of supervisor's school."

"Top of the class?" Duncan asked. He tilted his head slightly as he looked at McGraw, clearly reassessing him. "Well what have you learned in your studies about clearing out the homeless and the panhandlers and the hookers from a neighborhood?"

Here we go. McGraw cleared his throat to buy himself some time as he tried to think of a diplomatic answer. "Honestly, sir, what I learned is that homelessness and panhandling are complex quality of life issues. They require an intelligent approach. Sometimes we can take prostitutes off the street for loitering, but it usually takes plainclothes Vice Squads to sever the connection between the prostitutes and their customers, thus keeping the streets clear of that kind of activity."

Duncan crossed his arms. "And what about the guy who wanted to sell me marijuana?"

"Honestly, we would need a plainclothes Narcotics Unit to go after him."

Duncan looked puzzled by McGraw's responses. After a few moments of silence, he shook his head and told McGraw, "I don't like people who use the word 'honestly.' To me, it usually means everything else they say is a lie." He turned from a dumbfounded McGraw back to Gus. "Why did I come here tonight, Gus?" he asked. "It sounds like Sgt. McGraw can't help me at all."

"Like I said, Mr. Duncan, this is Sgt. McGraw's first night," Gus said apologetically, although he looked somewhat taken aback as well. "He and I will discuss this later."

Duncan turned back to McGraw. "Sergeant, you look like a nice, capable young man. Before I go, will you just promise me that you will handle this? Just promise me that everything's going to be fine, so this old man can get some sleep at night."

McGraw looked straight ahead for a few moments. *Wow, that was a quick mood change!* he thought. *Duncan basically called me a liar, and now he's back to asking for my help.* Moreover, McGraw worried, how could he make such a promise? Finally, he stammered, "I don't like to make promises beyond my power to deliver. But I *can* promise you I'll work with the lieutenant and do my level best."

Duncan didn't say a word. His face registered disgust as he spun on his heels and started walking towards the door. Gus followed him without a word, his uniform looking oddly casual beside Duncan's tailored tuxedo. McGraw was still staring after them in disbelief when Hitchcock appeared at his side.

"I saw Lurch point in my direction when he was talking to you before that Duncan guy spoke to everybody," Hitchcock said without preamble. "What did he say about me?"

"Lurch?"

"Yeah, that's what we all call Gus," Hitchcock replied, smirking. "He looks like that tall, creepy doorman, Lurch, from the old *Addams Family*."

McGraw was in no mood to be diplomatic. "Lurch, as you call him, warned me that cops like you are career-killers for their sergeants. He told me to be careful with you, which I already knew."

"Ouch," said Hitch, looking hurt. He backed up a step. "I thought we were friends."

Now McGraw was really annoyed. "Don't pretend that I don't really know you, Hitch. You complain about getting written up, but I know firsthand how many write-ups you deserved and never got when we were up in the Northeast." McGraw shrugged. "Maybe you've changed, learned a few lessons, but until I'm sure about that, yeah, I'm going to try to be careful around you."

To McGraw's surprise, Hitch didn't come back with a defensive retort. Instead, he looked at the floor for a few seconds, then slid his gaze to the doorway on the other side of room, where Gus and Duncan were talking quietly. Duncan seemed angry and impatient, and Gus was apparently trying to calm him down.

"You know what that's about, don't you?" Hitchcock asked, glancing back at McGraw. He seemed desperate to make himself useful. "Lurch is coming up on his twenty years. He wants to retire and get a cushy corporate job somewhere, maybe head of security for Duncan or one of Duncan's buddies."

Hitch stroked his chin in a meditative manner. "That's the plum that Duncan is dangling over Lurch's head right now. If this convention doesn't go right, that's the end of Lurch's dreams for retirement."

McGraw's first shift hadn't even officially started yet, and already the politics of this new job were making him queasy. Another glance across the room showed him that Duncan and Gus were chatting amicably now. Gus was smiling, and he shook Duncan's hand before the chief came and escorted Duncan out of the building.

Then Gus turned around, and the smile drained from his face as quickly as though someone had poured a glass of icy water over his head. He shot a glare in McGraw's direction and motioned him to come over.

"Uh-oh," commented Hitchcock. "Lurch doesn't look too happy."

CHAPTER 3

Convention Clean Up

"They told me you were a college boy, that you know how to talk to people," Gus told McGraw in a tight voice.

McGraw sighed as he followed Gus back to his desk. "I was trying to be honest."

Gus sat and dropped his hands palm-down onto the desk's surface—a little more forcefully than necessary, McGraw thought.

"Guys like Duncan don't want to hear that kind of honesty," Gus said, sounding somewhat condescending. "*I* don't want to hear it from you, either. When I tell you to do something, I want to hear you promise you'll do it."

Although he hadn't been explicitly invited to do so, McGraw lowered himself into the battered chair on the opposite side of Gus's desk. "You and I haven't had a chance to discuss this convention," McGraw said. He avoided responding to Gus's last statement on purpose. "You know Sector Three much better than I do. Do *you* think we can deliver on what Duncan wants?"

Gus looked across the desk from beneath furrowed brows. "Doesn't matter," he growled. "Do I have to explain everything to you?"

When McGraw didn't respond, the older man rolled his eyes toward the ceiling, and McGraw felt his muscles began to tense. Forcing his body to relax, he reminded himself that this was only his first day (well, night), and that things would get easier. *I hope.*

"Look, I want you to promise me you'll handle it, so once I've got your promise, you're telling me that you're on the hook if you fail," Gus continued as though explaining how the world worked to a child. "Then I know you'll be busting your hump to get it done. But if you don't promise, if you *won't* promise, that tells me that you're not even going to try."

Gus leaned forward with a scowl. "You're just going to screw it all up and leave me holding the bag. Didn't you learn anything up in Northeast or in that fancy new supervisor training?"

"I promise I'll look around the sector tonight," McGraw replied, doing his best to keep his tone neutral. He was gamely trying to offer reassurance without compromising his integrity. "I'll come back with a list of what I think we'll need to clean up the area."

"Make all the lists you want, but keep 'em to yourself," Gus replied. "We've got nothing more to put into your sector. You gotta work with what you've got." He chuckled, but the sound didn't convey amusement.

"I don't understand," McGraw persisted. "If this is so important, why won't the department give us added personnel?"

"It's political," Gus explained. "That's why Duncan got so hot talking to us. He's frustrated. The mayor thinks the Chamber of Commerce should pay for additional cops during the convention, and the Chamber thinks the city should pay. It's a standoff, so we have to plan within our means."

Great, more politics, McGraw thought. Aloud, he asked, "Can we redeploy inside the division? I see on the detail where my sector has only ten officers, even on weekend nights, when the other sectors are a lot quieter during first watch and they have twelve officers or more. Can I at least get a few extra bodies for convention week?"

"You need to get your hearing checked." Gus leaned back in his chair and scowled as if he'd been challenged. "I already told you that you're going to have to work with what you've got."

Gus glared at McGraw for another moment, and then his expression softened. "You need to know something," he said. "The chief wants us to use Sector Three first watch for disciplinary purposes only. Every house needs a toilet, he says. I can't assign just anyone to Three. It sends the wrong signal. Now, maybe if I catch someone in another sector screwing up, and he's already working first watch anyway, I can give him to you for a few weeks."

"Thank you," replied McGraw, who was not feeling thankful at all. "I really appreciate it."

"Glad you appreciate it," Gus replied in a mocking tone. He handed McGraw a manila file folder. "Here's something I'd appreciate if you would do for me. Hitch says you're pretty handy with computers. I need to do a presentation for Duncan's Chamber of Commerce committee. When things slow down later in the morning, take a look at what I've written and see if you can put it into one of those laptop slideshow programs."

McGraw rifled through the papers in the folder without really looking at them. His mind was racing. Gus had already told him to stay out on the streets tonight. Now Gus was also telling McGraw to design a computer presentation for him. Union rules forbade ordering sergeants to do work off the clock, but McGraw knew immediately that this presentation was something he'd have to work on at home.

"Now, promise that you'll do this for me," Gus said.

"You bet," McGraw responded automatically.

A sadistic smile spread across Gus's face as he stood up. "You're learning, college boy," he said. And he disappeared down the corridor.

Chapter 4

First Shift

After his frustrating meeting with Gus, McGraw looked around for Hitch. Despite the fact that his old coworker wasn't exactly a model cop, McGraw knew it would be helpful to have the perspective of someone more familiar with Sector Three on his first night. But Hitch was nowhere to be found, and McGraw couldn't get ahold of him on the radio, either. *Guess I'll be going out alone.*

McGraw started the shift by driving down Market Street, past the gigantic, darkened convention center. The streets were vacant except for a few people who walked with the wandering, shambling gait of people with nowhere to go and nothing to do. Some of them were homeless, some weren't, but all of them had the ragged, thinned-out look that caused the cops to nickname them *skels*—skeletons. Aside from those people, the only other sign of life McGraw noticed was a convention center security guard sitting at a desk behind a plate-glass window on the corner of Market and Grant. McGraw made a mental note to get in touch with that security post. *Someday, one of my officers might need assistance from the guard behind that desk.*

At Grant Street, McGraw turned left and headed north toward the back end of the convention center. There he saw two more ragged men picking through the convention center's dumpster. He made another mental note. *If they put in extra lighting and gates, those dumpsters will probably be left alone.*

As McGraw approached the intersection of Grant and Walnut, the streets began to come alive with bars, fast-food joints, an all-night pharmacy, and three night clubs that were authorized to stay open until 4 a.m.—two hours past bar closing time. Neon lights and the muffled thump of dance music flooded the sidewalks, which were far from deserted. Late-night revelers made their ways in and out of the clubs, and several knots of people were gathered in secretive conversations underneath awnings. There were even a few less-cautious panhandlers who stood near the street corners and accosted everyone who passed.

As he looked around, McGraw got a sense for just how big the job facing him was going to be. He knew that only a block down were a pair of convention center hotels, which meant that every conventioneer would have to walk through this area of intoxicated misbehavior every evening. This was probably the area that worried Herman Duncan the most. *I wonder which of these guys approached Duncan and tried to sell him weed*, McGraw thought as he scanned the area's inhabitants.

At the edge of the entertainment district, McGraw spotted one of his sector's patrol cars, stopped in the street with its light-bar flashing amber. Standing behind a nearby parked car was officer Melody Williams, writing out a ticket. When McGraw pulled up beside her, Williams raised her head and shot him a worried look.

"Is everything okay?" Williams asked. "Am I doing something wrong?"

"No, I'm just learning the territory," replied McGraw. He turned slightly in his seat and propped his elbow on the car's windowsill. "Looking around on my first night."

Williams looked relieved as she gestured to the red paint on the curb. "Stopping is prohibited here," she said.

"Did you run the tags yet?" McGraw asked her, peering at the car in question. It was bathed in a garish neon green thanks to a nearby liquor store's sign.

"Nope," she told him.

To McGraw, Williams seemed a little defensive. But before he could respond, a radio request came in from the Sector One sergeant. "McGraw? It's Jenkins. We need your patrol wagon for a job in Sector One, okay?"

"10-4," McGraw radioed back. "Take it. It's Ramsey and Somers," he said, remembering Gus's breakdown of the officers in Sector Three.

Williams looked back up from her clipboard and raised an eyebrow at McGraw. "You're loaning out our wagon?"

McGraw nodded. "It's a favor. Someday Jenkins will do us the same favor when we need it."

"But the bars haven't closed…" she began before McGraw cut her off.

"You were about to tell me why you weren't running the tags here," McGraw reminded her. It was department policy to run the tags whenever possible, because some illegally parked cars might have been stolen.

Williams pursed her lips, then stepped closer to McGraw's cruiser. "I've been told to write tickets," she began. "I used to run the tags, but the computers are slow at night, so I'd end up taking more time on each ticket." She fiddled with the clipboard for a moment, then continued. "Lurch complained about my lowered activity, and then my sergeant threatened to write me up. So I don't run the tags anymore."

"Run the tags," McGraw told her. "I'll handle…Lurch." The more McGraw learned about Gus, the less he liked him. And the more he enjoyed calling him "Lurch."

With even more to consider, McGraw went back to prowling the streets. Williams was on his mind especially. *Most patrol officers are a lot like her*, he thought. *They do what they're told, almost to a fault. That's how one bad supervisor can spawn ten bad patrol officers.* Feeling discouraged and angry, McGraw forced himself to turn the thought around in his mind, telling himself that Williams's compliant attitude also represented an opportunity. If she were so willing to follow bad orders, perhaps she'd be just as compliant with good ones, too.

Before McGraw could take that line of thought any further, though, a call came in from Hardy. *The guy who used to be plain-*

clothes Narcotics, McGraw reminded himself as he listened to the scratchy voice on the other end of the line. Hardy was investigating a reported domestic disturbance in Pleasantville. McGraw radioed that he'd be there for backup.

"No need for backup," was Hardy's terse reply. McGraw wasn't sure he'd heard correctly. Hardy couldn't possibly be telling his sergeant to not back him up.

"On my way," McGraw radioed, putting the car into gear.

Within a few minutes, McGraw came upon Hardy's car parked in the middle of a narrow tree-lined side street. Neighbors were out on the porches of their bungalow houses, craning their necks to see what was going on. Even in the dark, McGraw could tell as he got out of the cruiser that most lawns in the neighborhood were overgrown. There was litter strewn on some of them, and the yard next to the call address was filled with rusting auto parts. In comparison, the house at the call address looked fairly neat. The wooden steps had a fresh, unchipped coat of paint, and it looked as though the lawn had been mowed not long ago.

Hardy was standing outside the house, waiting for McGraw. At the top of the stairs was the silhouette of a man peering out through the screen door.

"You want this; you want to be here?" Hardy asked McGraw, disbelief clear in his voice.

"For backup?" McGraw asked. "Yeah, you need backup. Don't make me explain why it's dangerous to do domestics without backup."

"All domestics are dangerous," Hardy growled, turning his back to the house. "That's why I don't want the guy at the top of those stairs to feel like he's getting ganged up on. We already know he's angry. Two cops barging into his house might make him even angrier."

Despite the fact that Hardy's explanation made a certain kind of sense, McGraw was unmoved. "On my watch, two cops go to domestics," he said. "Always."

Hardy scuffed his shoe against the sidewalk, his frustration clear. "I just never know whether the guy backing me up will keep his cool."

"Take the lead. I'm just backup. Let's go." McGraw was tired of waiting.

As they turned to mount the steps, the man at the door called out, "No problem here, officers." Hardy and McGraw could hear sobbing inside the house, though.

When they reached the door, Hardy was polite but direct with the man. "I'm Officer Hardy. This is Sergeant McGraw. Would you mind stepping outside onto the porch?"

"I would mind very much," the man said in an exaggerated, indignant tone. There was an obvious slur in his speech. "You have no business being on my porch."

"We had a request for service, sir," Hardy told him. "We can't leave until you step outside and we speak privately with your wife."

His bravado dissipating, the man lowered his head and shuffled through the door. Behind him, McGraw could see a tiny woman with a large pile of hair on her head. Her eyes were red from crying.

"May we come in, ma'am?" Hardy asked. She nodded.

The interior of the small house was fairly clean and neat, but when McGraw looked through the archway to the dining room, he spotted a beer can on the table and another crushed can lying on the floor.

Hardy took the woman aside. "Did your husband strike you, ma'am?" McGraw noticed that the other officer bent down to look her straight in the eyes. Hardy was searching for an indication of whether she was really afraid, McGraw realized. It was a technique he himself had learned from a veteran officer years earlier, but he'd never before seen another cop use it.

"N-no," she stammered. "But he threatened to. So I got scared and dialed 911. But now I'm sorry I did. Please don't take him away, okay?"

After hearing the woman out—but without answering her question—Hardy went back outside with the husband. McGraw sat down at the kitchen table with the wife and began filling out a domestic incident report. As he wrote, he could hear Hardy on the porch.

"That's my sergeant in there," Hardy said to the man. "He expects me to lock you up for the night because it's standard procedure." There was a slight pause. "But I don't want to lock you up. That's just going to make more trouble for everyone, including me and the sergeant. So I need you to tell me that there will be no more trouble here tonight. Promise you'll go upstairs right now and sleep it off. That way you get to sleep it off in your own bed, instead of in our lockup, which smells really bad this time of night."

There was another, longer pause as Hardy waited for the man's response, which McGraw couldn't make out.

Hardy continued. "Now, I'm going to promise you something. I'm going to remember this house, and I'm going to keep an eye on you both. Treat your wife right. Get yourself some help. I'll be back one of these days, just to check up on her—and to check up on you, too."

McGraw shook his head as he finished up the paperwork. Hardy was old school. This was no longer the proper procedure for handling domestic disputes in Central City. Two years earlier, right here in Pleasantville, a man had murdered his girlfriend less than an hour after police had been at their house. The woman had told police she didn't want to press charges, even though the man had punched her in the jaw. Twenty minutes later, the same cops were dispatched back to the house on a report of multiple gunshots. After that night, it became department policy, with rare exceptions, to lock up every suspected abuser on a domestic call.

McGraw heard Hardy's footsteps start down the wooden stairs. When he had presumably reached the sidewalk, Hardy paused and called out to McGraw, "We're done."

After reminding the woman to call 911 if she felt that she was in danger again, McGraw caught up with Hardy. "Hold on a sec." McGraw felt he had to discuss the situation before he and the other officer left the scene.

"So you're comfortable with this?" McGraw asked as they walked toward their cars. "About not calling a wagon for him?"

"I've been working Pleasantville for a year," Hardy told McGraw. "You see the condition of this house, this yard? This is a working man. We lock him up, and then he doesn't make it to work in the morning. He loses a day's pay. Maybe he loses his job." Hardy ticked off the possibilities on his fingers. "Then maybe he gets charged with assault because Lurch wants to show some activity for this sector. Then the guy's got a criminal record, so he can't get another job. Is all that going to be good for his wife? You think that will make him less angry with her?"

McGraw wasn't sure how to respond to Hardy's tirade. "It's not procedure..." he began, but Hardy interrupted him.

"So call the freakin' wagon!" Hardy almost shouted. "You're the supervisor on the scene. Technically, you're breaking procedure, *not me*." Hardy stepped into his patrol car, slammed the door, and drove off.

Feeling stunned, McGraw opened his own driver's side door and looked up at the house. The man and woman were standing together in the front doorway, probably wondering what would happen next. McGraw threw himself down behind the wheel and thought for a moment. Hardy was a good cop—at the very least, he clearly cared about *people* and wasn't simply checking off the correct boxes—but he was also brazenly insubordinate.

How do you supervise someone like that? McGraw didn't have a clue. He gunned the engine and took off down the street.

Minutes later, a call went out from another Sector Three officer reporting a drunk and disorderly arrest at Grant and Walnut. "Tahiti Lounge, 326 Grant, D and D, request backup and a wagon."

McGraw radioed Ramsey in the Sector Three patrol wagon, but it was still tied up in Sector One. *No problem.* McGraw radioed dispatch to request a wagon from another sector. To his surprise, all he got was silence. *Now* that's *a problem.* With no other options, he radioed Ramsey again and gave him the Tahiti Lounge address. "Come as soon as you can. We need you."

The scene in front of the Tahiti Lounge was chaos when McGraw pulled up. Hitchcock was in the middle of it, with the arrestee cuffed and pressed up against a wall. Two other patrol officers were restraining a group of men who were barking out threats at the man under arrest. And, of course, there were dozens of people on the sidewalk watching. Some were yelling encouragement to the angry men being held back.

"What's going on, Hitch?" McGraw asked after he'd shouldered his way through the crowd.

"This genius spilled beer on one of their girlfriends," Hitchcock said, jerking his head toward the man in handcuffs. "When they asked him to apologize he made a lewd remark about her. I happened to be here, so I saw most of it go down."

McGraw didn't bother asking what Hitchcock was doing at the Tahiti Lounge at 1 a.m. He got on the radio to Ramsey in the wagon. "How's it looking?" Ramsey reported the wagon was free now, but that he and Somers were at least 30 minutes away.

"We gotta get this guy outta here," Hitchcock commented as he looked around at the pandemonium, which showed no signs of dissipating. "Where are Ramsey and Somers with the wagon?"

"They're on the other side of town," McGraw told him in a tight voice. "They had a job in Sector One."

"You loaned out our wagon before bar-closing time?" Hitchcock looked incredulous.

McGraw didn't respond. Clearly, he had a lot to learn about his new sector. "This crowd is getting ugly," he said, stating the obvious. "Let's put this guy in the back of a patrol car."

The nearest cruiser belonged to Cooper, one of the cops restraining the crowd. Hitchcock maneuvered the man toward the backseat, but the arrestee was so drunk he could barely walk. McGraw motioned for Cooper to come help, and within a minute, Cooper was driving the prisoner back to the district drunk tank.

"I couldn't find you earlier, Hitch," McGraw said as they watched Cooper's taillights disappear down the street. "Now you say you were here when this whole thing started. What's going on?" He was annoyed about not being able to find Hitchcock at the beginning of the shift, but he tried not to show it since he had already been harsh to the other officer after the incident with Herman Duncan.

"I'm working a case that could be pretty big," Hitch confided. He glanced around to make sure no one else was listening. "I'll tell you about it, but please keep it under your hat for now."

"Hitch, I wasn't able to reach you at all. That should never happen."

Instead of apologizing, Hitchcock launched straight into telling his story. "The head of security at the hotel down the block is ex-police, an old buddy of mine," he began. "We both worked the Southeast. Two weeks ago, he calls me in and shows me a surveillance video from the hotel lobby. Here's a pretty young lady entering with a middle-aged guy who's staggering drunk."

McGraw frowned and watched the sidewalk outside of the Tahiti Lounge to make sure that no more trouble was brewing. "So what's the case?"

"Forty-two minutes later, the video shows the pretty young lady leaving by herself, walking fast," Hitch continued. "In the morning, the guy comes downstairs to talk to my buddy behind the hotel desk. He's a conventioneer, flew here from Denver. The pretty lady put him to bed and then ripped him off." Hitch laughed and shook his head. "She took his wallet, with cash, all his cards, and his driver's ID. He's a married guy, a family man with small children, so he doesn't want to report a crime. He just wants his ID so he can get back on the plane and fly home. He hoped that my buddy, you know, might know the woman, might know how to get his ID back."

"What?" McGraw was genuinely surprised. "He thought hotel security might be in on something like this?"

"No, but he knew that sometimes hotel security gets acquainted with the local working girls," Hitchcock explained. "But not my buddy, and not this hotel." The neon lights threw lurid shadows across Hitch's face as he narrowed his eyes. "My buddy wants to nail the girl and whoever she's working for. Turns out the Denver guy met her here, at Tahiti Lounge. So I'm making inquiries, very discreetly."

Ah, there it is. McGraw turned to face the other man. "We have to turn this over to the detective bureau," he said. "You can't get to the bottom of this on your own."

"I'm not on my own," Hitchcock objected. "I'm working with my buddy and another guy at hotel security. He's also given me contacts at the other hotels. The Denver guy, father-of-the-year, is never coming back to make a statement, much less testify. So there's nothing for detectives to investigate."

McGraw didn't know what to say. Hitch was right. Without a robbery report from the victim, the detective bureau had no way of assigning a case number.

"McGraw, this case is my passport out of first watch," Hitch pleaded. He pointed at the Tahiti Lounge. "I've got to do this. Otherwise they're going to bury me here until retirement. This is my chance. You've *got* to let me stay on it."

McGraw sighed, wishing that the shift was over. What else was going to happen tonight? "Let me think about it," he told Hitch. "For now, get back on patrol. Answer some calls. Write some parking tickets. Show some activity, for crying out loud. Your activity sheet is going to look empty tonight."

Hitch nodded halfheartedly, although he continued to stare at the Tahiti Lounge.

Well, Hitch is a grown man. I've given him my advice; what he does with the rest of his shift is his decision. McGraw walked back to his car and radioed Cooper.

"Did you get back all right with our guest from Tahiti Lounge?" he asked.

"Yeah," said Cooper. He sounded sheepish. "But there was a problem, Sarge. The motion in the car must have gotten to him. He puked all over my backseat. A lot. It looks like a crime scene back there."

Of course. "I'll be right in," he said. "Go ahead and check out a relief vehicle to drive for the rest of your shift."

Thankfully, calls from dispatch had all but stopped for the night. McGraw parked in the lot and approached Cooper's patrol car. He held his breath, braced himself, and then opened the rear door. Cooper hadn't exaggerated. The seats and floorboards looked as though someone's stomach had exploded.

McGraw went inside the substation and filled out the paperwork to take Cooper's car out of service. He allowed himself a little extra time to clear some other papers off his new desk, including the domestic incident report, and then he took a look at Gus's folder. The notes Gus had made were minimal and his handwriting was like chicken scratch. *I figured he wouldn't make this easy,* McGraw thought wryly. He put the folder in his briefcase. *I was right—I'll have to do almost all the work on this presentation myself, after hours, on my home computer.*

Since it was so quiet, McGraw decided to go back out and learn some more about the streets in his sector. He had always liked getting to know the place where he worked, checking out the back alleys, the dead ends, the shortcuts. While on first watch in Northeast, he used to play a game with himself to test his knowledge. He would drive to the end of a block, stop the car, close his eyes, and try to imagine what he would see around the next corner. Then he'd open his eyes, pull forward, and see how many details he had recalled. Using this strategy, it didn't take long before he felt that he knew his sector like the back of his hand. In fact, there had been a few tense situations when detailed knowledge of that kind had come in very handy.

McGraw's aimless patrolling eventually took him all the way back to the Walnut and Grant area, which was now very quiet. The streets—still brightly lit but now deserted—were filled with trash and broken bottles, and they smelled of urine. McGraw made some notes about how to possibly avoid a repeat of this scene during convention weekend. Porta-potties, maybe? A late night sanitation crew? Could Duncan and the Chamber spring for any of these things? He could already hear Lurch shooting down every idea he had.

After brainstorming a few more minutes with no more luck, McGraw put his car back in gear and drove three blocks past Walnut and Grant. Abruptly, he hit the brakes. There was Hitchcock's patrol car, with all of its lights off, sitting under a tree in a small public park. McGraw shone his spotlight on the vehicle and saw Hitchcock's surprised face staring back at him. Then the passenger side door flew open, and a slim young woman in a skimpy black dress popped out and disappeared into the darkness.

Fuming, McGraw pulled up alongside Hitchcock's vehicle on the driver's side. Hitchcock rolled the window down and visibly steeled himself for what McGraw was about to say.

"What the hell was that?" McGraw had no other words for what he'd seen.

"It's that case I told you about," Hitchcock said, pasting an ingratiating smile on his face. "I'm working that case."

McGraw rolled his eyes. "Please tell me that's the only thing you were working on in there," he muttered, then glared at Hitch. "Come on, Hitch. A woman like that, in your car, at this hour? *Really?*"

"She didn't want to be seen talking to me," Hitchcock explained, holding his hands up in a gesture of surrender. "This is what we arranged."

McGraw just stared at Hitchcock. *If he's lying,* McGraw told himself, *he'll crack.* But despite McGraw's glare, Hitchcock continued to explain how the young woman in the black dress fit into his investigation of the robbery at the hotel.

Finally McGraw cut him short. "Hitch, this is the second time tonight I could have written you up, and we're not even finished with our first shift together. Earlier I couldn't reach you.

Now you've got a civilian in your cruiser. Is this going to be the story every night with you?"

"I am *not* your biggest problem in this squad," Hitchcock replied, slowly shaking his head. "Have you seen Cooper or Jackson in the last hour? I'm no rat, Sarge, but you should know that around this time each weeknight, as soon as the radio goes still, they usually go off and find a nice quiet place to sleep."

The truth was that McGraw didn't know where Cooper and Jackson were. He wasn't about to let Hitchcock know that, though.

"I'm just saying," Hitchcock continued when McGraw didn't respond. "You found me because I'm working, Sarge. I'm working this case. And if I crack this thing, it will be good for both of us. If we lock up a criminal ring that's ripping off tourists, Gus will be happy with us, and he'll even get to brag to Herman Duncan. Big win for everyone."

Still, McGraw said nothing. He held up a hand in a perfunctory wave, then put the car in gear and drove back to the substation. Along the way, he radioed for Cooper and Jackson. Each responded promptly enough, but did they sound groggy, as though they'd been sleeping? Maybe. He couldn't tell.

Back at the substation, a stack of paperwork awaited McGraw, representing all the night's activity. He had just gotten through the last of it when 6:30 rolled around. Jenkins, the Sector One sergeant who had borrowed McGraw's patrol wagon, stopped by his desk.

"Just so you know, Gus is really ticked off about the puke in Cooper's squad car," the sergeant said. "It's a five-day turn-around for cleaning, and that means we'll be one car short this weekend."

"It couldn't be helped," McGraw replied, resting his chin on his fist. "I had to loan you our wagon. Remember?"

"Yeah, well, you should never lend out your wagon before bar-closing time. Every sergeant knows that."

"I didn't," McGraw said, swallowing a much more unpleasant response.

"I know you didn't know," Jenkins said. He laughed. "That's why I asked you for it!" He stood to leave. "Now you know."

McGraw's first shift as a sergeant was over. He dropped his forehead into his palm. *Did all of that really happen in just eight hours?*

McGraw's wife, Peggy, called him during his drive home, eager to hear about his first night.

"Well, it ended with me getting sandbagged by another sergeant," he finished, after giving her the rundown using his car's Bluetooth feature. "So that's one more guy I know I can't trust in this place. Add him to the lieutenant who wants me to do his presentation work for him, and the real estate big shot who wants me to transform Grant Street into Disneyland within a month. It's been quite a night."

"How's your crew?" she asked.

"I'm already worried about roll call tomorrow night," McGraw admitted. "I don't know what to tell them. My best officer is insubordinate. My worst one is bending the rules right and left while he's playing Sherlock Holmes. There's another one who seems afraid of her own shadow. Two guys might be sleeping on the job. And these are the people I need to count on so we can get the whole sector cleaned up in four weeks." He sighed as he approached his interstate exit and flipped on his turn signal. "If I don't work a miracle, who knows how long they'll keep me here, stuck on first watch."

Peggy tried to sound helpful. "What about your supervisor training? Your criminal justice classes?" she asked. "And those classes you took on police supervisory practices for seven weeks. Didn't they give you any methods that could help?"

"Maybe," McGraw said. In reality, in all his years of criminal justice schooling and police training, he'd never had an hour's worth of formal preparation for this new role as leader of a ten-officer squad.

"You'll figure it out," Peggy told him, sounding a lot more confident than McGraw himself felt. "You did so well on the sergeant's exam; you're bound to figure it out. Just take it one day at a time. It's just ten people, right? How hard could it be?"

CHAPTER 5

Neighborly Advice

As soon as he returned home McGraw took a catnap, but the fact that he wasn't yet used to a nocturnal lifestyle combined with lingering stress from his shift meant that he wasn't able to stay in bed very long. The sun was up, and so was he.

I might as well make myself useful. With that thought, McGraw put on a pair of old sneakers and went downstairs to look at a drip in the kitchen sink. After a few minutes of craning his neck at awkward angles while crouched beneath the sink, McGraw was able to see what the problem was. However, repairing it required a plumber's wrench, which he didn't have. *I'll drop by a neighbor's house to borrow one.*

Stanley Sabato and his wife, Margaret, had been next-door neighbors to the McGraws for the past two years. They'd been the first to welcome the young couple to the neighborhood, and Stanley soon made a habit of lending McGraw shop tools that the younger man hadn't acquired yet as a homeowner. During the holidays, the Sabatos brought Italian pastries to Adam and

Peggy from their favorite markets in the city, as well as little presents for the McGraws' daughter, Naomi.

After the short walk next door, McGraw wasn't surprised to find Stanley in his garage, which was the envy of every other amateur handyman and landscaper on the street. As usual, the yard tools hung along one wall in a neat row, longest to shortest: leaf rake, garden rake, hoe, long-handled shovel, and garden spade, all of them well used but clean. The lawnmower was swept free of grass clippings.

"You sure like things neat," McGraw said by way of compliment after Stanley had found the necessary wrench in a bright red tool chest.

"I come by it honestly," Stanley offered with a smile. "Twenty-six years in the Navy. It's the best way to operate, if you want to be efficient. On a ship with limited space—and sometimes with lives at stake—you want to be efficient."

McGraw nodded. He couldn't argue with that logic.

Stanley pulled a pruning hook from the end of the row and examined it. He was not a big man—his head, with a thick but neatly trimmed shock of white hair, didn't come up to McGraw's shoulder—but he exuded a calm energy. He never hurried and looked as if he could keep the same steady, deliberate pace for days on end. Stanley had dark eyes and serious crow's feet, and McGraw had no trouble imagining him squinting out from the bridge of some ship.

"You have to know what assets you have—gotta be able to see them at a glance—if you're going to use the right tool for the right job," Stanley continued as he put the pruning hook back in its place.

For some reason, Stanley's comment about tools made McGraw think of his misfit patrol officers. If these faulty cops were his assets, his instruments, how would he ever learn to deploy them in a way that maximized their strengths and compensated for their weaknesses? *Maybe Stanley can help me with this problem too—even though it'll be a lot harder to tackle than a leaky sink!*

McGraw turned the plumber's wrench over in his hands a few times and asked, "Stanley, have you ever been in charge of people? Like in a managerial or supervisory role?"

"Sure," Stanley replied. "Except the Navy calls it leadership, not supervision."

"What's the difference?"

"Short answer?" Stanley asked as he walked toward McGraw holding a bottle of oil. "Supervision is about stuff. Leadership is about people." While McGraw held the wrench, Stanley put oil on the ratchet.

"Don't they overlap?" McGraw asked, directing his comment toward the top of Stanley's bent head. "Supervision and leadership?"

"Sure. Lots of leaders have to be concerned with physical assets—stuff—in addition to their people," Stanley responded. He straightened up and put the cap back onto the bottle of oil. "But you can be a supervisor without being a leader."

"Because you just deal in stuff?" McGraw guessed.

"Because you just deal in stuff, or because you treat your people like stuff," Stanley clarified as he wiped his hands with an old towel. "That's why I never took to this idea of referring to human beings as 'assets,' as if they were printing presses or forklifts."

Just then, Stanley's wife, Margaret, opened the door that led from the garage into the utility room.

"Would either of you home improvement heroes like some coffee?" she asked. "I just made a fresh pot."

McGraw's eyes were feeling grainy due to his lack of sleep, and he eagerly accepted the coffee and Stanley's invitation to sit in the sunny breakfast nook off the kitchen. From his position in the Sabatos' comfortable wicker chair, McGraw could see through the window into his own backyard, where an autumn wind had cracked a thick limb on a pin oak tree. His own pruning hook lay on the patio outside. *I'll get to that job eventually*, he thought with a twinge of guilt as he considered Stanley's impeccable yard and well-cared-for tools.

For the next fifteen minutes, McGraw told Stanley about his first day as a sergeant in Midtown East. Stanley listened, posed a few questions between sips of coffee, and nodded sympathetically from time to time. Finally, McGraw finished his story and sat back in his chair, causing the wicker to creak. He hoped Stanley would give him advice about Hitch or Hardy, and maybe some tips about how to rein them in. Instead, Stanley asked a simple question.

"What did you say you wanted to do about all the lapses in procedure that you saw on your first night?"

"Well, I was going to write a memo restating the importance of procedure," McGraw replied. When Stanley said nothing, McGraw added, "Put it in writing, you know, so no one can say they didn't know."

Still nothing from Stanley. The older man appeared to be studying something in the bottom of his coffee cup.

"Um...so...what do you think I should do?" McGraw was really starting to feel uncomfortable.

"Heck, I don't know," Stanley said, placing his coffee cup on the table. "I've never been in law enforcement. But in the Navy that's a real cover-your-ass approach. You can show your supervisors that you issued a memo, so now every deviance from procedure is not your fault."

McGraw nodded. That *had* been his strategy.

"But tell me this," Stanley continued. "Did anyone follow procedure properly on the first night?"

McGraw thought back on the shift. "Most of them did. Most of the time."

"What about you?"

McGraw remembered the domestic disturbance call with Hardy, during which he had let the husband stay at home instead of taking him in. Then there was his decision to put the drunk in Cooper's patrol car. He wasn't even sure if that squared with standard procedure.

Stanley smiled, his crow's feet crinkling up. "It's a yes-or-no question, hotshot."

"No," McGraw admitted, feeling sheepish. Then, "I cut a few corners."

Stanley nodded as though that had been the answer he was expecting. "Well then, to start, if you're going to write a memo about doing things by the book, you have to do things by the book yourself. But I don't even know if you *want* to do that. It sounds like there are lots of gray areas in policing. The people under you will take their cues from you, and what you do is more important than all the memos you could write in a year."

"Right," McGraw said. Stanley had made a good point. *I'll have to think a little more carefully about the decisions I make and the example I set.*

"Next: no memo."

Stanley's latest instruction came as a surprise. "Why not?"

"Several reasons," Stanley replied. He held up one finger. "First, because the people who follow procedure don't need it. Sending it to them will be insulting. It tells them you didn't notice that they were sticking to procedure already."

Stanley held up another finger. "Second: You deviated from procedure, so you can't ask other people to stop doing it, at least not without admitting that what you did was a mistake. But I don't even think you consider it a mistake."

Stanley lifted a third and final finger. "Third, and this is the most important reason: The people who need this message the most will probably ignore the memo anyway."

McGraw frowned. "Why would they do that?" he asked.

"They'll think you're not really serious about this, because writing a memo is a chicken way of handling it." Stanley smiled to take the sting out of his words.

McGraw thought about what he had heard for a few seconds. Stanley had convinced him that the memo strategy wasn't the right way to proceed. He would have to think of a Plan B. "So, how do I reach them? The people who need to hear what I would have put in the memo?"

Stanley smiled again. "After you get yourself in gear, you talk to them individually."

McGraw sighed, feeling frustrated. "Well, it seemed like all I did last night was confront them individually about these issues. They either ignored me, walked away from me, or in Hitch's case, he tried to talk me into his way of thinking."

Stanley held up a hand. "Did I say 'confront'? That word has a bad reputation. I said 'talk to them.' Politely. Assume that they want things to run as smoothly as possible, just as you do."

Immediately, McGraw could think of at least one thing that wouldn't be running smoothly in the near future no matter how many people he talked to. "What about the fact that I loaned out the wagon and put a prisoner in Cooper's squad car...who then puked all over the backseat?"

Stanley grimaced at the mental image, then asked, "Have you fixed the problem?"

McGraw shook his head and pushed down a wave of anger at the Section One sergeant. "We're going to be short one car all weekend while Cooper's car is getting cleaned."

"Well, you screwed up, and everyone knows it." Stanley shrugged. "Nothing to do but say, 'I screwed up.'"

"Okay," McGraw agreed, but he didn't relish the prospect. He could clearly picture Hardy smirking at him.

"But you're not the only one who should have thought of this, right?" Stanley asked, absently tapping his fingers on the tabletop. "I mean, these people have been around. Someone else might have reminded you to not loan out the wagon."

McGraw was feeling sheepish again. "Right. Williams mentioned it. I didn't listen."

"So you've got to let them know that you rely on them to help you anticipate problems like this," Stanley replied. "And that means, when they come up with an idea, you've got to listen."

"Of course," McGraw agreed, as if it were the most obvious thing in the world. Privately, he wasn't sure he wanted to contemplate the ideas his new squad might come up with.

"Here's something else to remember," Stanley continued. "When people are upset, it's harder to listen to them."

"Why is that?" McGraw was starting to feel that his brain was reaching information overload, but it was clear that Stanley wasn't close to being finished with the discussion. In fact, the other man's voice took on a lecturing tone as though he was a teacher and McGraw was his star pupil.

"Well, let's say you work for me, and you're upset about what you think is some lame-brain decision I've made," Stanley said. "In a situation like that, as soon as you open your mouth, I go into a defensive mode and my wheels are turning, trying to come up with an answer. So instead of listening, I'm concentrating on what I'm going to say, thinking about how your argument doesn't hold water, thinking about what a jerk you are and how wrong you are about me."

"Oh," McGraw murmured, recognizing a bit of himself in the description.

After taking in the look on McGraw's face, Stanley stood. "Let me get the coffeepot and refill your mug," he said. "Then I want to tell you a story that might help you."

Soon, fresh steam was rising from both men's mugs. Stanley settled back into his chair and began to tell his tale. "When I worked in the Pentagon the first time, I did a study about how we could keep better inventory of airplane repair parts as they moved from the manufacturer to Navy warehouses. I'd gone out and looked at some technology, new at the time, that the big package-shipping companies use now—hand-held scanning devices and all that jazz. I became an in-house expert of sorts."

Stanley paused to take a sip of his coffee. "Whew! That's hot." He wiped his mouth with the back of his hand. "Anyway, so one morning the admiral I work for tells me to go talk to this other staff about my work, because they're looking at a similar system and need some advice. I head over there with my little briefcase, thinking that I get to be the good guy, help somebody out."

A rueful smile touched Stanley's lips. "But the guy I'm supposed to brief attacks my work even before I start presenting. He starts complaining about how the study was put together and how my data was flawed. So I'm already ticked off. Then his boss, another admiral, comes into the room, and the meeting starts."

Stanley took another, more cautious sip from his mug. "But I'm so focused on this guy's criticism—which was unfair—that I can't really concentrate. All I kept thinking was, *You jerk. You must have some hidden agenda here. Why don't you want this project to succeed?* I used all my brain cells thinking about what this guy had said and how I was going to rebut, and I had none left to brief the admiral. As you can imagine, it wasn't a very impressive briefing."

McGraw nodded.

"My point is, that same thing can happen when you're trying to listen to someone who's upset, or is attacking you or your decision. You use all your brainpower mounting a defense, or thinking about what a jerk that person is, and you have none left over to listen, to understand the person's position." Stanley paused and looked McGraw in the eye. "You *have* to listen so that you can ask good questions."

Stanley stood, walked to the counter, and motioned toward a covered plate of pastries. McGraw declined, which didn't stop Stanley from choosing one for himself.

"You said you've got to turn around this crew pretty quickly, right?" Stanley asked before taking an impressive bite from his cream cheese danish.

"The convention is coming in four weeks," McGraw told him. "We're flying by the seat of our pants."

Stanley took another bite of danish. "Did you ask the people on your team, or whatever they call it in law enforcement, for help? They might have some ideas." He held up a finger. "And if they come up with the idea themselves, they're more likely to get behind it when you're trying to make it happen. They'll own it. The whole lot of them could pull together."

"I wish I could get Gus to hear what you're saying," McGraw muttered, staring down into his coffee cup.

"I doubt if he even knows he needs help." Stanley demolished his pastry with one more bite, then stood and put his plate into the dishwasher. "Do you know what Gus wants from you?" he asked after he had returned to the table.

"I know exactly what he wants," McGraw answered. "He wants me to impress Herman Duncan and make him happy about the convention. But he's shooting down every idea I have for getting it done. So in that sense, I don't know how he wants me to handle this. It's a mixed signal from him."

Stanley nodded sympathetically. "It's frustrating when you're not sure what the boss wants, that's for sure. My question for you is this: Does your team know what *you* want?"

McGraw didn't have an answer for that one. After a few quiet seconds, he said, "The task seems impossible. I don't know what to do, or how to get it done, so how can I get them to help me? The fact is, I don't know what I want, not really."

"Well, that's something, anyway," Stanley said, smiling. "It's not the million-dollar answer, but it is, at least, the million-dollar question."

"Thanks for the advice, and for the plumber's wrench—and for the coffee," McGraw said, standing and shaking Stanley's hand. "Any chance I could entice you to come into the city for a visit to Midtown East sometime next week? The hours are kind of crazy, but if you came at the end of the shift, around 6:30 or 7:00, we could maybe have a little leadership talk over breakfast at the Windsor…if you're willing."

"Breakfast at the Windsor sounds great," Stanley replied. "You buying?"

PART TWO

CHAPTER 6

The Breakfast Club Meets Again

The next Tuesday morning Stanley showed up at 7:00 a.m. sharp, dressed in a blazer and tie. He was more formal by several degrees than any other civilian in the substation that day, and his attire earned him several curious looks. Now off the clock, McGraw showed his neighbor around and introduced him to several of the civilian employees and uniformed officers who had just come on for second watch.

McGraw had hoped that all of his officers from first watch would be gone by the time Stanley arrived, but Hardy was still there, filling out some paperwork at his desk. As McGraw approached Hardy to introduce him to Stanley, Hardy looked up at McGraw and asked, "Did anyone tell you we still have the old forms, the old arrest report forms?"

McGraw narrowed his eyes and shook his head. This was the first he'd heard about arrest report forms.

"It's the coding," Hardy explained, turning to Stanley and including him in the conversation, even though the two men hadn't been introduced. "Any day now, our arrest forms are going to get kicked back to us because the forms are out of date and the coding is wrong. Then they'll want us to sit down and recode these reports all over again. "

McGraw suppressed a sigh. "Does Gus know about this?"

"Who knows what he knows or doesn't know?" Hardy shrugged, then leaned forward with a scowl. "He'd know if he were a lieutenant in Narcotics, I can tell you that. This would never happen in Narcotics."

McGraw was still trying to understand what was going on. "So you're telling me you haven't mentioned this to Gus?'

"I'm mentioning it to you," Hardy responded with a note of belligerence in his voice. "I'm following chain of command."

"Okay," said McGraw. He was tired and didn't want to address the other man's rudeness, especially not in front of Stanley. "I'll ask him about it next shift." Hoping to leave the substation soon, McGraw introduced Hardy to Stanley and the two men shook hands. But just as McGraw was about to tell Hardy to have a good morning, the former Narcotics officer spoke up again.

"Here's another thing we need," Hardy said. "A police bike. For bicycle patrol."

"You want to be a bike cop?" McGraw asked, raising his eyebrows. He was genuinely confused.

"No," Hardy said with smirk. "The bike is for you. So you can put on some shorts and ride around on it next time you lose a patrol car for a whole weekend."

While McGraw gaped, Hardy gave a half-wave to Stanley. "Nice meeting you," he said, and walked off without saying anything else to McGraw.

Before anything else could happen, McGraw led Stanley out of the substation, and the two men walked the three blocks to the Windsor Hotel. They sat at a table beside a big window that looked out on Second Street. It was a brilliant sunny day, but a steady autumn wind rattled the glass.

"See what I mean about Hardy?" McGraw asked after they'd been seated and served. "Big fan of mine. He looks at me as if he's surprised I can get myself dressed in the morning."

"He might be a tough nut to crack," Stanley admitted. "I can see that." He dug into his egg-white omelet.

"Look, I'm glad he mentioned the forms," McGraw went on. "You can bet that no one else would have told me. But the way he said it, he made it sound like I'm an idiot for not having known about it already." He speared a chunk of fried potato with a fork and dipped it into the small dish of ketchup on the edge of his plate with a little more force than was strictly necessary.

"That little scene he made wasn't about forms or coding," Stanley commented, wiping his mouth with a paper napkin. "It wasn't even about being short a car for the weekend."

McGraw looked up from his plate. "Then what was it about? What did you hear him say that I didn't hear?"

"Try repeating exactly what he said."

Stanley wasn't making idle chatter, and McGraw didn't even mind being quizzed, especially if it helped him deal with Hardy. McGraw was more than a little worried that Hardy's attitude might start to infect the other members of his squad. He thought back to what had happened earlier that morning.

"Hardy complained about the forms being out of date, and how much work it will be if the main office sends them back to us and makes us reenter all the codes on the new forms."

"Okay," Stanley said.

"And he's still annoyed with my screw-up on Cooper's car, wants to let me know what a dumb mistake it was," McGraw continued.

Stanley picked up his coffee and took a swallow. "Anything else?"

McGraw thought for a moment. "Those were his complaints. Today. He'll probably have more tomorrow."

Stanley leaned back in his chair and stroked his chin. "Did you hear him say, 'This would never happen in Narcotics'? I imagine that's what this is *really* about."

McGraw sighed. "Yeah, but comparing the Narcotics Unit with patrol is like comparing apples and oranges. Narcotics is an elite unit. They don't have nearly the volume of incident reports we have, and their report processing isn't automated like ours." He looked down and scooped some scrambled eggs onto his fork. "If he's going to hold Midtown East to Narcotics Unit standards, then he's going to be angry and disappointed a lot."

"It's not about the reports or the forms," Stanley corrected. "It's about what Narcotics represents to him. As you say, it's an elite unit. Do you know what position he held over there?"

McGraw swallowed his eggs and shook his head. "I heard he was pretty important to his squad, even though in rank he was just another officer," he explained. "He and the chief over there got fairly close, and Hardy went out on a lot of special jobs."

"Then what?" Stanley prompted.

"Then he and the chief had a falling out and he ended up here." McGraw chuckled mirthlessly. "In the crapper."

"You told me he also lost his eligibility to take the sergeant's test when he was transferred," Stanley continued. "Is that right?"

"That's right," McGraw confirmed. "He would have been promoted in the same sergeants' class as me."

"And that all got yanked away from him because he ticked off his last boss."

McGraw paused in the act of lifting a sausage link to his mouth. "I see what you mean," he admitted.

"It's good that you see, because in a minute we can talk about what you might do about Hardy. First, let's talk about what you should do about Adam McGraw."

"Huh?" McGraw grunted as he swallowed his food. Then, more clearly, "What do you mean?"

"Somebody as smart as you should have figured all this out when you met Hardy," Stanley chided. "In fact, you should have anticipated he was going to be a problem from the start."

McGraw saw what Stanley was getting at. "So I need to work on those listening skills, like in the story you told me about the Pentagon briefing."

"Bingo," Stanley said with a grin. "You have a pen on you?"

McGraw pulled a pen from his shirt pocket. Stanley slid a clean paper napkin across the table.

"Number one: listening."

As McGraw wrote it down, a thought occurred to him: *This is the leadership class I never had. Who'd have thought I'd learn this much over coffee with my neighbor?*

CHAPTER 7

Notes, Napkins, and New Ideas

"What else did we talk about the other day?" Stanley asked McGraw after taking another bite of his omelet.

McGraw looked up from his napkin and clicked the pen closed. "Uh…you asked me if I knew what Lurch wanted, and I said no."

Stanley just nodded. It was a sure sign—as McGraw had learned in their first conversation—that there was more to the answer. "And…" he prompted.

"I asked if you knew what Gus wanted, and you said no, not really," Stanley recalled. He held up a finger. "First of all, you should stop calling him Lurch, unless you're going to call him that to his face."

McGraw grimaced and took a sip of coffee to hide his embarrassment. "Everyone calls him Lurch," he muttered.

"Yes, but you're not everyone," Stanley replied, sounding like a disappointed father lecturing his child. "You're in charge. If you mock the boss, you send a message to your team that you're the kind of person who will talk behind someone's back. They gotta figure it's only a matter of time before you're saying stuff about them."

"Okay," McGraw agreed, even though he wasn't quite convinced. *It's not like I'm the one who came up with the nickname,* he told himself. But a small voice in his head told him that Stanley was probably right.

Stanley cleared his throat. "Anyway, you told me you didn't know what Gus wanted, and I asked…" He trailed off.

"You asked if my team knew what *I* wanted," McGraw supplied.

"Write that down," Stanley instructed, pointing at the napkin.

Obediently, McGraw wrote, "WHAT DO I WANT?" on the napkin.

"Now let's talk about your team and your responsibilities. Do you have a job description? Something written down?" Stanley inquired.

"It's a very specific list," McGraw told him. He scooped the last bite of scrambled eggs off his plate while he tried to remember the official language. "Supervise activities of subordinates. Assign staff in work schedules. Disseminate policies. Analyze activity reports." He stopped. "The rest is too long to remember."

Stanley thought for a few seconds. "So you've got to accomplish the mission of your unit, to use a Navy term. Oversee sector patrol, book activity, respond to calls, transfer detainees. And then all the other tasks that support these activities."

McGraw nodded. "Right."

"That it?" Stanley looked across the table with a quizzical expression on his face.

McGraw suspected that the other man expected him to have more ideas as to what his job entailed, but all he could think of were small, mundane tasks. He shrugged and admitted, "I'm not sure," then wrote "JOB DESCRIPTION" on another napkin so that he'd remember to read and think about the official description later.

"Okay. What about 'assign staff in work schedules'?" Stanley asked. "How do you assign staff?"

"Okay, well, I assess what everyone is best suited for and make sure they do that," McGraw answered. At the expectant look on Stanley's face, he continued, "Ramsey and Somers are big strong guys who can really handle the wagon, so I make sure they're out there every night on the wagon…"

Stanley interjected before McGraw could continue listing the other officers on the squad. "Are there other officers who'd like to work the patrol wagon?"

It was a question McGraw had never considered. "I guess," he answered. "Wagon work can get very intense sometimes, but it's easier in some ways, too. You still have to patrol and respond to some calls, but the wagon is never called first, because we can't risk tying it up."

Stanley raised his eyebrows. "So why not let more people take turns in the wagon?" he asked as he reached for the creamer.

"Because I thought being efficient meant getting the best people suited to the task," McGraw answered, feeling a little confused.

"A lot of the time it does," Stanley agreed. "But efficiency isn't your only concern. At least, it shouldn't be your only concern," he clarified. "How often do Ramsey and Somers patrol alone in their own squad cars?"

"Not very often. They do a good job on the wagon, and frankly, I don't know who else is trained to drive the wagon or haul prisoners."

"So what happens if Ramsey or Somers gets sick or transfers out tomorrow?"

McGraw was beginning to feel like he was in the middle of a test, and that he had forgotten to study. "I haven't been in this job long enough to think of that," he said. "I guess I'd have to work the wagon myself and train someone."

"And then you're not able to supervise the way you're used to supervising, so everything in the squad that night is a little out of whack," Stanley speculated as he stirred his coffee.

"I guess so," McGraw agreed. *There's so much I haven't even thought about yet. What else am I missing?* he wondered.

"On a Navy ship, sometimes people get hurt or even die when things are out of whack," Stanley offered. "I'll bet police work is the same."

McGraw nodded. "You're right about that."

Stanley leaned forward. "Here's something to consider," he said. "When people are successful at their work, it makes them happy. But keeping people in one area with no chance to move, or excluding other people because you don't want to take the time for them to learn, those are bad ideas. You've got to find a balance between putting people where they'll succeed and helping them stretch their capabilities a little bit."

McGraw clicked his pen open and closed while he thought. "So I should give one of the wagon jobs to someone who hasn't done it before?"

"I'd say you should let someone ride with either Ramsey or Somers." Stanley paused and passed his empty plate to the server who had stopped at their table, then continued. "Someone who's expressed an interest in doing it. That way you give either Ramsey or Somers a chance to learn how to teach, and it lets someone else in the squad have a taste of a job that might be more interesting than patrol."

McGraw looked down at the table, where he'd spread two napkins. On one, he'd written "LISTENING" and "WHAT DO I WANT?" On the other, he'd written "JOB DESCRIP-TION" but nothing else.

"What do you call that?" he asked as he considered his notes. "Letting people learn different jobs?"

"Put that under the heading 'Development,'" Stanley replied. "You've got to develop your people. That's part of motivating them, and it's also part of improving the team."

McGraw thought about what development might look like in his squad. "I have an officer, Melody Williams, who Lurch says isn't good for anything but writing tickets."

Stanley quirked an eyebrow. "What do you think?"

"She's expressed an interest in doing more, but I haven't responded," McGraw replied.

"And how ready is she?"

"Good question," McGraw commented. "Maybe I'll have her ride for a week or two with Somers. I think he'd be a better teacher than Ramsey."

McGraw wrote "DEVELOPMENT" on his second napkin, then jotted "IMPROVE TEAM" below it. He shook his head— the writing was bleeding through the napkin and becoming illegible.

Stanley leaned forward to look at the notes and said, "We should get you some paper and get a little more organized about this."

CHAPTER 8

More Lessons in Leadership

After McGraw paid the check, he and Stanley walked back to the substation. McGraw led Stanley to a second-floor conference room that was hardly ever used, figuring it was as good a place as any to continue his informal education on leadership. Stanley took a seat, and McGraw shut the door behind them. Every once in a while, someone walked to the door and peered through the glass panel at the two men, but no one interrupted.

"Let's talk about your job first, in a large sense," Stanley began.

McGraw flipped open the legal pad he'd snagged from his desk and placed it on the table in front of him. He had the same feeling he'd had in school when, early in a semester, he figured out that he'd landed with a professor who had a lot to teach him.

"What is leadership?" Stanley asked.

McGraw laughed. "Boy, you weren't kidding when you said we're talking in the large sense." Then, "Let's see. I guess leadership is when you get other people to do things."

Stanley nodded. "What things?"

"Uh…the things you want them to do?" McGraw winced inwardly. *What a lame answer.* But Stanley was nodding again.

"Good," he said. "Dwight Eisenhower said that leadership is when other people do what you want them to do because they want to do it."

McGraw frowned as he tried to mentally sort though the quotation. "I'm not sure I follow," he said.

"Well, there are three kinds of leadership," Stanley explained.

McGraw began to take notes as Stanley spoke.

"There's leadership from authority: the do-this-or-I'll-break-your-legs kind. Then there's leadership through motivation: the do-this-and-I'll-give-you-that kind. Then there's inspirational leadership: that's where people buy into the leader's plan and the organization's goals, and they do things because they really want to do them."

McGraw looked up after he had stopped scribbling. "And that's the best kind, right?"

"Well, there are times and places for all of these things." Stanley glanced through the room's window into the hall. "It seems to me there's plenty of the first two kinds of leadership in this department, don't you think?"

"Sure," McGraw agreed. "Most things run on a do-it-or-else authority basis. But supervisors also get what they want by offering favors or withholding them. That's what they'd call motivation."

Stanley raised a skeptical eyebrow. "And what do you call it?"

McGraw thought briefly of how Gus had told him that the chief wanted to use Sector Three first watch "for disciplinary purposes only" and grimaced. "Manipulation. Game-playing," he answered. "I hate it. Makes me feel like a child, having lollipops held over my head. But I figure the best I can do is try to get used to it."

"So," said Stanley, "in this department's culture, where you've already got plenty of authority and so-called motivation, maybe inspirational leadership is an area of opportunity. It's something worth working toward because it doesn't happen naturally."

Stanley stood and walked to a whiteboard that hung on a sidewall. He motioned to a column of numbers and asked, "Can I erase these?"

"Go ahead," McGraw told him. *They've probably been here longer than I have.*

After taking a few swipes with the eraser, Stanley picked up a marker and wrote "LEADERSHIP" near the top of the whiteboard, then filled in some bullets below the heading:

- INFLUENCE
- OPERATE
- IMPROVE

"Okay," he said, putting the cap on the pen and turning to McGraw. "A leader has to influence people, operate to accomplish the mission, and improve the organization, got it?"

"Got it," McGraw murmured as he copied Stanley's notes onto his legal pad.

Stanley continued, "Influence means you gotta provide three things." He wrote out, "PURPOSE - DIRECTION - MOTIVATION" beside the first bullet point.

"What do you think this one means?" he asked, tapping the board next to "PURPOSE."

McGraw thought for a moment. "They have to know why they're doing something?"

"Sure," Stanley confirmed, walking a few steps closer to the conference table. "And it would be helpful if your people also thought that it was a good idea or for a worthwhile cause, whether it's having the best ship in the fleet or having the best substation in the force."

"There's not much chance of that, Stanley." McGraw held his hand out toward the hallway window as though showing off just how subpar his substation was.

Stanley's gaze followed McGraw's, and he nodded. "Well then, how about best squad in Midtown East?"

"That could be a goal, but a stretch goal, for sure," McGraw told him.

"Good. I'll take it. How about this one?" Stanley asked, walking back to the whiteboard and pointing at "DIRECTION."

"That means you have to tell your people what to do," McGraw said.

"Not exactly, or at least not in every case," the older man explained. "I mean, if you have someone who's really experienced, you're not going to give them detailed instructions about how to make a traffic stop or fill out an arrest report, right?"

"No," McGraw agreed. "That'd be insulting."

"Right. That's micromanaging. For most people, it's better to tell them what you want to have happen and let them figure out how to get it done," Stanley said. "Obviously, this is a sliding scale. The most inexperienced team members need more guidance than the most experienced, and chances are that everyone else falls somewhere in between. Your job is to figure out how much guidance to give."

"So you can give enough," McGraw thought out loud as he wrote down the essence of what Stanley had said.

"So you can give them *just* enough so that they're challenged," Stanley clarified. "It's like you're always putting things just beyond their grasp. That's how people learn."

Once McGraw had looked up from the legal pad again, Stanley pointed to the last component of "Influence." "How about this one? MOTIVATION."

"That's a big one, isn't it?" McGraw guessed.

"Absolutely," Stanley confirmed with a decisive nod. "What do you think motivates people? Why do people work? More important, why do they work hard, put in a little more effort to really nail something?"

"The obvious answer is money and promotions," McGraw said. "And that's the big problem with police work. The laziest, most careless patrol officer gets paid the same as the best officer." He fiddled with the edge of the legal pad, rolling and unrolling the corner of the top sheet. "In fact, he can make more money than a good officer if he knows how to play the overtime game right. And if that bad officer is also good at taking tests, he'll climb the ranks and make even more money. Which means there's a good chance he'll stay on the force longer than a lot of the good officers."

Stanley smiled when McGraw ran out of steam. "That's a pretty grim picture you're painting."

"Maybe I'm exaggerating a little," McGraw admitted. "But I know that if I could reward the best officers with more money, my job would be so much easier."

Stanley shook his head slowly. "Actually, most surveys show that employees rank 'more money' way down the list of the things they want from their work. So maybe money doesn't matter as much as you think."

McGraw looked a little skeptical, so Stanley continued. "Did you get a raise with your new responsibilities?"

"Yeah. Peggy and I went out to celebrate. We had a nice dinner in a restaurant that didn't give out crayons with the place mats," McGraw recalled with a chuckle.

Stanley laughed too, then asked, "Did your raise, those extra few bucks, make the difference between you being happy or unhappy? Is that what you were celebrating—you got a raise, so now you're happy?"

"No, of course not," McGraw answered, shaking his head. "I guess we were celebrating the fact that I'd earned sergeant rank. I'd been recognized with a new promotion and new responsibilities."

"So what if you'd taken the sergeant's test, and your only reward was the raise?" Stanley asked. "No promotion. No new responsibilities. You stay where you are. They just throw you a few more bucks."

"That would have been nice, I guess," McGraw said, stroking his chin as he thought. "But it wouldn't have been the same. I wanted the money, but I felt ready for more responsibility, too."

Stanley wasn't finished yet. He walked to the table and rested his hands on the back of a chair. "So let's say they doubled your pay or tripled it," he continued. "But they kept you as a patrol officer in Northeast forever, never promoted you. They paid you very well but refused to recognize your true abilities. Would that have kept you happy until retirement?"

"No, of course not," McGraw answered without hesitation. Then, more slowly, "I never thought of it that way."

"Right," Stanley said, looking pleased. "Workers always rank recognition above pay when they talk about what makes them happy at work. They also rank autonomy higher than money. People want to have control over what they do."

McGraw laughed. "Lots of people think cops have too much autonomy already," he observed. "What other job lets you drive around all night, armed and unsupervised? We can stop any car or any person that gives us reasonable suspicion that they're up to no good. That's a lot of autonomy."

Despite McGraw's description of police work, Stanley didn't look convinced. "What about that officer you told me about?" Stanley snapped his fingers a few times as he searched his memory. "Ummm...Williams. Yes, that's the one. The one writing parking tickets."

"What about her?"

"You said that Gus told her not to run auto theft checks on the tags," Stanley reminded McGraw. "Then you ordered her to start running the checks again."

"So?"

"So, where's her autonomy?" Stanley moved to the front of the chair and sat down so that he was on eye level with McGraw. "She's worried about her productivity and the computers at night are slow. She told you that. But you told her to run all the tags." He raised his eyebrows. "Do *you* have any idea how slow the computers are? If they get really slow, do you want her standing around forever, waiting for one single tag to clear?"

McGraw took a long breath as his misstep sunk in. "I see what you mean," he told Stanley. "If I had told her she should run the tags when she can, I'm still giving her direction. But I'm letting her figure out the details of how and when it's a good use of her time to do it. So she would feel more autonomy than if I told her to always run the tags, right?"

"Now you're getting it," Stanley smiled. He looked proud. "There's more to it than that, of course, but you're grasping the basics."

Just as McGraw was starting to feel pleased with himself, he saw a blur of movement out of the corner of his eye. He turned, feeling his good mood deflate. Hardy's face was at the window beside the door.

CHAPTER 9

A Heart-to-Heart with Hardy

Suppressing the urge to groan in frustration, McGraw motioned Hardy inside the conference room. As soon as the other officer had closed the door, Stanley greeted him warmly.

"Hello, officer," he smiled. "Why don't you join us?"

Hardy shot a glance toward the whiteboard at one end of the room, narrowed his eyes briefly, and then addressed himself to Stanley. "I just wanted to ask the sergeant about possibly rescheduling my days off next week."

Funny how Hardy is so much more polite and subdued now that he wants something from me, McGraw thought.

"We're having a little chat about leadership," Stanley explained, ignoring Hardy's stated reason for entering the conference room. "It would be great if you could join us." He motioned toward a chair on the other side of the table.

"Oh yeah?" Hardy asked, crossing his arms and making no move toward the chair. His politeness disappeared. "What's McGraw taught you so far?"

Stanley ignored the dig at McGraw. "We were just talking about what motivates people," he explained.

"That's easy," Hardy said without missing a beat. "It's respect. People are motivated when they get proper respect from their supervisors." With a movement so small McGraw wasn't 100 percent sure he'd seen it, Hardy jerked his head in McGraw's direction. "But respect is in pretty short supply around here."

Swallowing an angry retort, McGraw looked down at his papers. He had been enjoying Stanley's company, but with Hardy in the room, he suddenly felt the urge to get up and leave.

"I couldn't agree with you more about the importance of respect," Stanley commented.

McGraw looked up from his notes to see if Stanley was being sarcastic. The older man was nodding in apparent sincerity. *The traitor*, McGraw thought.

"So what—specifically—is bugging you?" Stanley asked Hardy. There was nothing confrontational in his voice. He was being completely charming, much to McGraw's chagrin. *Whose side is he on, anyway?*

"What's bugging me?" Hardy counted on his fingers as he spoke. "You already heard about the out-of-date forms. Then there's this building, which is so dilapidated it's not fit for livestock. The district chief is never around when we need him, so we're stuck with Lurch." He rolled his eyes toward the ceiling. "What else? Well, most of the other officers in my squad are here because they are either bums or screw-ups. The worst of the bunch," he paused and looked at McGraw, "is off running his own investigation with his sergeant's approval, because apparently he and the sergeant are buddies."

There was no doubt that Hardy was talking about Hitchcock. *I can't believe that Hardy assumes Hitchcock is getting favorable treatment!* McGraw fumed to himself.

"What else?" Stanley asked.

McGraw turned his head toward the back wall of the conference room to hide his expression of disgust. *Seriously? How long is Stanley going to encourage this guy to complain?*

Hardy's voice lost some of its stridency. "And, I'm still hot about getting pulled from the Narcotics Unit. But I probably shouldn't say anything more about that, because talking too much is what got me in trouble."

Feeling curious despite his frustration, McGraw turned back around. "Why do you say that?" he asked. He had only heard about Hardy's story secondhand and had never discussed it with him. "Tell us what happened at Narcotics. It won't go any further than this room."

"I thought," Hardy began, "that I was close enough with the chief there to give him some constructive criticism. I wanted to let him know about some mistakes he was making, and how those mistakes were reflecting badly on him among other people in the unit." Hardy paused and shifted his feet. "I guess I assumed that leaders rely on their closest friends to give it to them straight. I thought I could be that friend to the chief."

"What went wrong?" McGraw asked. He was beginning to feel the stirrings of real sympathy for Hardy. *I certainly know what it's like to have a boss who needs to clean up his act.*

"I misjudged my chief," Hardy explained. "He took everything I said as a personal attack. He stopped talking to me, ignored me for weeks, walked right past me in the hallways. Then, all of a sudden, I started getting written up on my smallest deviations from procedure. I was getting called out on every little technicality, every mistake. The complaints piled up until I was out."

Stanley gave a low whistle. "That would definitely get to me," he commented. "Would that get to you, Adam?"

"It would," McGraw admitted. "In this department, if your supervisor wants to take you down, he can always find a way. If he wants to hurt you bad enough, he can get Internal Affairs after you. It might take eighteen months for them to figure out you're innocent, but by then the damage is done."

Hardy gave McGraw an assessing look and his expression softened. "So you know how it goes," he said.

McGraw just nodded.

Stanley broke the silence. "We were just discussing how much McGraw needs your help," he said, motioning toward the chair a second time. "He'd like to be able to rely on your experience to help him make the most of what everyone here is capable of— though I understand you don't think they're capable of much."

Hardy searched Stanley's face for a sign that he was being mocked. Once he realized that the older man was utterly sincere,

Hardy moved around the table and sat on the edge of the offered chair. "I have a few ideas," he said, catching McGraw's eye. "Maybe I'm taking a risk here, but I'll tell you right now that I think you should be very concerned about Hitchcock."

"I appreciate that," McGraw told the other officer. "You know, he's not my pal. Not by a long shot. Yes, I knew him in Northeast, but that's where I learned to stay away from him. I was disappointed to find him here. I'm doing what I can to contain him." McGraw allowed himself a half-smile. "Like an oil spill."

"If I were you, I'd bury him with writing parking tickets and put Williams on something else," Hardy advised, then looked down at the table. "I'm sorry if I'm out of line."

"Not at all," McGraw told him. "I'll think about that."

Hardy shook his head, then looked up and smiled at McGraw for the first time.

"If you're serious about wanting my help, I've got some ideas about the convention weekend. But I'd like to make some calls and check out a few things with some friends of mine. Give me until Friday and I'll have something for you." Hardy got up to leave.

"Wait, what days did you want to reschedule when you came in here?" McGraw asked, holding up a hand.

"Forget it," Hardy said as he opened the conference room's door. "Not a problem." And with that, he left.

Answers and an Assignment

After the door had closed behind Hardy, McGraw turned to Stanley. "That went surprisingly well."

"Under MOTIVATION, make a note about listening," Stanley instructed, the skin beside his eyes crinkling as he smiled. "All Hardy wanted was to be heard. Once you heard him out, he was so motivated to help you that he forgot all about wanting to change his days off."

"Yeah, I don't understand that part," McGraw said, frowning as he wrote. "If he came in needing some days switched, why would he change his mind just like that?"

"My guess is that he didn't really need any days switched at all," Stanley explained. "He was trying to exert some autonomy in a job where he feels he has none. You heard how he felt when his boss stopped talking to him." Stanley caught McGraw's eye. "I get the sense you've been avoiding him, too."

"You're right about that," McGraw admitted, feeling a little ashamed. "I've been giving him a wide berth. But in my defense, those snide comments were wearing me down."

Stanley laughed. "Know what the real kick in the pants is going to be? I'll bet Hardy comes up with some really good ideas, and you wind up adopting some of them."

If Hardy has some ideas that are helpful, I wouldn't mind that particular kick in the pants at all, McGraw admitted to himself.

Meanwhile, Stanley had walked back to the whiteboard. Apparently, class was back in session. "What about this one?" he asked, pointing to the next bullet point: OPERATE.

"I guess that means you've got to get the job done. Make your numbers, keep everyone happy up the chain of command," McGraw ventured, pushing Hardy out of his mind for the time being.

"You've got to do all of that," Stanley said, "and you've got to do it in line with your personal values and the organization's values. And now, assuming you don't have any questions about operating within values, that just leaves us with IMPROVE."

"You're talking about improving the organization, right?" McGraw asked.

"Right. Your squad should be in better shape when you leave it than when you came on board," Stanley said. "You improve the organization by working on the systems, but also by improving the individuals. That's development."

McGraw scribbled more notes as Stanley continued to talk.

"You've got to look for ways to keep people challenged, look for new tasks that will stretch their abilities. You've got to think about what the next challenge is for each person. It's like juggling a bunch of different lesson plans in your head."

"You know, Peggy teaches fourth grade," McGraw commented, drumming the legal pad with the tips of his fingers. "I've heard her talk that way about challenging her kids, by making a separate plan for each one of them. But I never thought the same approach would apply to leading a squad of patrol officers."

"Children are just small people," Stanley chuckled. "We don't stop wanting to grow and be challenged once we reach adulthood. Great leaders understand that."

McGraw leaned back in his chair. "Did they really teach leadership this way in the Navy?" he asked. "It doesn't sound very military to me."

"They did and they still do." Stanley looked unmistakably proud.

"This police department seems so different from the military," McGraw mused. "It's rare that people here want to be challenged. A lot of them want to get into top units like Narcotics and SWAT, but once they feel stuck in patrol, it's like they lose interest."

He paused for a few moments to get his thoughts in order. "Now I'm wondering if the problem is the patrol chain of command. Maybe the bosses aren't challenging the patrol officers, which is why all the best officers want to get into special units." It was an interesting—and potentially game-changing—thought.

"There's more to it, though," Stanley told McGraw. "Everyone in the Navy knows they need to grow. If you don't grow, if you don't move up the ranks at a certain pace, the Navy has no place for you." He jerked his thumb toward the door in an unmistakable "get out" gesture. "You'll get discharged. That's the deal. You either move up or move out."

McGraw absorbed that, then shook his head. "Oh, but now we're talking about two completely different kinds of organizations," he told Stanley. "In this department, in most police departments, you can remain a patrol officer your whole career. Never excel. Never grow. You can get away with doing the bare minimum and never risk losing your job unless you really screw up badly."

"I'm familiar with the job protections that civil service gives the police," Stanley replied. "And you know what? I think it makes leadership inside the police department *more* important, not less. In the Navy, even a weak leader can get good results since so many subordinates are self-starters intent on moving up."

McGraw was silent for a moment, feeling a weight of responsibility that hadn't existed a few minutes ago settle onto his shoulders. "I didn't think of that."

"The way you describe your police department, it sounds like good leadership is essential to good results in patrol," Stanley observed, crossing his arms. "If a patrol leader can't inspire the squad to do more than the bare minimum, then that might be all they produce in terms of results. The bare minimum."

Stanley capped the marker and dropped it into the tray below the board.

"Remember the million-dollar question?"

"Sure," McGraw said as Stanley walked back to the table. "What do I want from my team?"

"If you could tell them that—what you want from them—it would give them a real head start on knowing how to work for you," Stanley explained. He dropped into the chair, which responded with an alarming creak. "You've got to let your team know what you believe in, what's important to you, how you want to operate. In a way, it's like giving them a look at the compass inside you, the thing that keeps you on course."

"I should tell them outright, 'This is what I want'?" McGraw asked.

"If you tell them what you believe in, then you can derive other things from that, like what everyone should be doing on a day-to-day basis. And if you tell them what to expect, they can hold you to it," Stanley answered.

McGraw picked up his pen and held it poised over the legal pad, but he didn't write anything down. "I don't know that I've ever sat down and tried to articulate something as broad as 'what I believe in,'" he admitted.

"Most people never do," Stanley said. "But if you're in a leadership position, with other people dependent on you, a leadership philosophy gives you a strong foundation for the decisions you make. It helps guide your interactions with people up and down the chain of command. And if you stick with it, your squad will see that you're consistent. More than anything, people need consistency from their leaders."

McGraw shot the older man a smile. "I know I do."

"Consistency matters a lot," Stanley continued. "Nothing ruins morale on a team faster than a boss who says one thing and does another."

Stanley's description hit close to home. "That's Lurch—I mean Gus," McGraw blurted out. "He's famous for changing his mind and not owning up to it. The first few times, it makes you mad. Then you learn not to count on him at all, for anything."

"So, Gus aside, what do you—Adam McGraw—know about leadership?" Stanley asked. "What do you believe?"

"Talk about your open-ended questions!" McGraw chuckled, shaking his head.

Stanley laughed too. "Just tell me a story. Part of your job as a leader is to be a teacher. Good teachers tell stories."

"Yeah, but so do thieves, Stanley," McGraw countered. "So do weasels like Hitchcock. Eight years of policing has made me fairly suspicious of storytellers. There's an endless stream of b.s. artists in this job, inside and outside the force."

"Obviously I don't want you to tell bull stories," Stanley clarified, holding up his hands in mock surrender. "But you've just confirmed how powerful stories are by telling me how easily they're misused. What I'm really getting at is that if you use stories—if you talk about people making choices and taking actions in real-world terms instead of talking about concepts and theories—your squad will understand you more easily. They'll also be more likely to remember what you told them."

"Why is that?"

Stanley leaned back in his chair and put his hands behind his head, fingers interlaced. "What did the three little pigs use to build their houses?"

McGraw paused to see if Stanley was joking. When the other man's benign smile didn't slip, he answered, "Straw, sticks, and bricks."

"And what was the moral?"

McGraw thought for a second, then grinned. "Uh, look out for wolves coming down your chimney?"

Stanley rolled his eyes. "Try to be serious."

"Right," McGraw said. "The little pig in the brick house survived because he built the better house. So the moral is to take the time and effort to do things right the first time."

"See? People remember stories," Stanley replied, looking pleased with himself. He reached across the table for McGraw's legal pad. "Now, here's some homework."

On a blank page of the legal pad, Stanley drew a vertical line from top to bottom, right down the middle. Atop the left-hand column, he wrote "BEST," and over the right-hand column he wrote "WORST."

"Over the next day or so, I want you to think of the best leader you've ever worked for, and I want you to write down what made that person the best. Then, think of the worst leader you've ever worked for, and write down what made that person so bad," he instructed, handing the pad back to McGraw.

"You mean, what they *did* that made them so bad?"

"Just tell their stories," Stanley replied. "What they did, the choices they made, and what values they expressed in those choices. Also, what kind of skills they had or lacked, both technical and interpersonal. When you finish that, we'll talk some more."

Stanley stood and buttoned his blazer. McGraw grabbed his legal pad, then walked his neighbor to the substation's door.

"Thanks for coming," McGraw told Stanley. "I learned a lot today."

"Good," Stanley said, reaching out to shake McGraw's hand. "I like teaching, so this was fun for me, too. I'm going to dig around in my papers when I get home. I have something to show you that may help."

"What's that?"

"Well, I went through this drill—writing a leadership philosophy—a number of times when I was in the Navy, and I'm sure I still have my notes and stuff," Stanley said as he pulled his keys from his pocket. "When I find them we'll look at them together."

Chapter 11

Jenkins's Warning

After watching Stanley get into his car, McGraw found himself deep in thought as he walked back down the hall. Stanley had given him so much to think about, and had caused him to question a lot of the things he had previously taken for granted, about police work specifically and leadership in general. In fact, McGraw was so preoccupied that he almost ran into Sgt. Jenkins after turning a corner.

"Whoa!" Jenkins exclaimed, stepping back. "So who's the geezer in the snappy sportcoat?"

McGraw decided to ignore Jenkins's "geezer" remark. "That's my neighbor, Stanley," he explained. "He's retired Navy, and he's just giving me some pointers on supervision and leadership."

Jenkins looked surprised. "What's he telling you about? Motivation, training, development? That sort of thing?"

McGraw nodded. "Partly, yeah."

"And he thinks it would be smart to apply military ideas inside this department?" Jenkins raised his eyebrows, clearly skeptical.

"You don't?"

"I was in the military, McGraw, unlike you," Jenkins said in a tone of voice that bordered on patronizing. "And believe me, this ain't the military. For one thing, the bums and slackers in the military have no job security. They can't hide behind civil service rules like our bums and slackers. That's only one difference, but believe me, from a supervisor's standpoint, it's a big one."

"There's no doubt in my mind that you're right," McGraw replied, stepping to the side so that another officer could pass in the narrow hallway. "But Stanley knows all about civil service too," he continued. "He says it might make good leadership that much more important in policing. He's got me wondering if some of the cops we think of as bums and slackers really want to do well, but they're just frustrated and cynical, you know, because of poor leadership."

Jenkins looked down the hallway, which led to the main meeting room. A fairly steady stream of officers and other employees walked in and out. "I don't doubt that most of these people started at the academy wanting to be good cops," he said, motioning toward the activity. "But it doesn't take long for even the dumbest ones to figure out how things really work. There aren't many rewards for doing well. So they figure it out pretty quick."

Jenkins began to list the components of his version of "how things really work" on his fingers. "Do the minimum you can get away with. Keep your head down. Keep your nose clean. Study for the promotion tests. Move up. Retire. Collect your pension. That's the way it is, and anyone who says otherwise is lying. Or they're naive, like Stanley."

A bit uncomfortable, McGraw scuffed his shoe against the linoleum floor. "I know what you're saying," he replied, choosing his words carefully. "But I came into this job with almost no preparation. These talks with Stanley are a big help. He compares leadership to having a kind of internal compass, you know? I feel like he's helping me find my bearings here."

Jenkins just stared for a moment, as though he were checking whether or not McGraw was really serious. "Look, McGraw, you seem like a good guy," he stated. "I know some cops who worked with you in Northeast, and they liked you a lot, unlike your buddy Hitchcock. But this stuff isn't going to help you make lieutenant any faster. So why don't you just stop trying to outflank the rest of us who have already been here a few years? You're just going to show us up and make more grief for everyone."

Taken aback, McGraw frowned. "This isn't about making lieutenant or causing you trouble," he said. "I'm talking to Stanley because I need help doing my job." *And I wish everyone would stop assuming that Hitchcock and I are best friends!*

Jenkins's expression softened, and he reached out to give McGraw's shoulder a friendly slap. "You should come to me," he said. "Or Ott, or Kelsey. We're the senior sergeants around here. You come to us with problems and questions. We've all done Third Sector at one time or another. We know the territory."

"Thanks," McGraw replied, meaning it. "I appreciate that." Jenkins had never offered to help McGraw before. Was he really that threatened by Stanley and the effect his advice might have? *Even if he is, I'm still going to learn everything I can from Stanley!* McGraw promised himself.

"And I hope you're not still sore that I took your wagon that night," Jenkins added, not quite meeting McGraw's eyes. "That was just a prank, you know? It was your initiation, and I owned up to it right away, didn't I?" He cleared his throat. "That should tell you right there that you can still trust me, right?"

"Of course it does," McGraw lied in a flat tone of voice.

Jenkins rushed on, clearly uncomfortable after McGraw's less-than-convincing reply. "Because I know all about this military-style leadership training that Stanley's selling you." He shook his head. "It won't wash. Not in this department. What you're doing is going to play out in one of two ways. Either the chief learns about it, gets all excited, and forces us all to do the same thing, which none of us wants, or…" Jenkins trailed off.

"Or what?" McGraw prompted.

"Or Lurch finds out what you're up to before you get too far," Jenkins answered, meeting McGraw's eyes once again. "In that case, Lurch will take that compass you're talking about and shove it down your throat, needle end first. Then your compass is going to wind up pointing you to a desk job on the road to nowhere."

Wow, Jenkins is really intimidated by Gus, McGraw thought. "Okay," he said aloud. "Thanks for the advice." He turned and began walking toward the stairwell, ready to start the homework Stanley had given him.

"Wait a second!"

McGraw turned around to see Jenkins hurrying toward him.

"Before you head upstairs, let me give you some more friendly sergeant advice, and listen to me good," Jenkins instructed in a stern voice. "No one gets in trouble or fired for doing nothing. As a supervisor, all this answering on calls and showing up at calls when you're not dispatched is going to get you a one-way ticket to Internal Affairs. And believe me, they'll literally beat all the motivation right out of you."

McGraw's eyes widened. He wasn't surprised by what Jenkins was saying—after all, this wasn't his first day on the job as a cop—but he *was* surprised that Jenkins was so vehement. *I wonder if Jenkins has some personal experience with Internal Affairs.*

"You are *never* right in Internal Affairs since their goal is to punish officers, especially supervisors," Jenkins continued. He was clearly on a roll. "I know too many Internal Affairs investigators who have made their careers and reputations on getting officers fired for the simplest things. No matter how right you are, you cannot win; you *always* lose in Internal Affairs. So, get in your squad car, find a nice place to sit, and wait until dispatch calls you directly."

Jenkins looked McGraw in the eye, and to McGraw's disbelief, actually began to shake his finger at him. "Stop responding to calls, stop being backup on calls, and for God's sake stop being so damn visible," he ranted. "Keep your name off of any reports, and anytime you do find yourself in a situation, write it up in a manner that puts the burden on someone else."

By this point, McGraw's jaw was hanging open. He had no idea how to respond to the other officer.

Jenkins took advantage of the silence to issue one last warning. "Heed my words, McGraw, or you will suffer in this department. Don't give anyone the rope to hang you with, because they will, college boy." Shooting McGraw one final stern look, Jenkins said goodbye.

McGraw stood in silence for a few moments as he digested Jenkins's warnings. He knew that Jenkins meant well, and that the points he'd made were based on reality. Still, McGraw couldn't quite reconcile himself to sitting back, doing nothing, and putting his best efforts toward not rocking the boat.

For now, I'm going to keep talking to Stanley and learn all I can, he thought. *Once I have a little experience here, I'll be able to see more clearly how his advice might and might not work in law enforcement.* With that, he began climbing the stairs.

PART THREE

CHAPTER 12

Best and Worst

After double-checking to make sure that the conference room was still empty, McGraw went in, sat down at the table, and took out the piece of paper with the side-by-side BEST and WORST columns. Without hesitation, he wrote "Wheeler" on the BEST side.

Mark Wheeler had been McGraw's high school football coach, and even though it had been years since McGraw had put on a jersey and helmet, Wheeler's name had still been the first that came to mind when Stanley asked about the best leader McGraw had known.

McGraw tapped the point of his pencil on the paper as he allowed himself to reminisce about his days as a high school athlete. After a few seconds, he wrote "concern for people" on the first line.

Coach Wheeler knew his players well. He knew who had a bruised muscle and needed more rest, who was sick, and who was having difficulty off the field, in class, and at home. At many big high schools like McGraw's, football players were often treated like disposable parts by coaches who were interested only in winning for the sake of their own glory. But Wheeler always treated his players like they were his own sons.

However, that didn't mean Wheeler was easy on the kids who played for him. So on the next line, McGraw wrote "tough," then smiled wryly as he thought about how he had discovered that aspect of his coach.

McGraw had been a 15-year-old sophomore with a bit of an attitude when he tried out for the varsity team. He had physically matured a little quicker than most of his classmates, and he'd been such a star on the junior varsity team in his freshman year that he assumed he'd soon be an All-American. During the first week of tryouts, his on-the-field attitude was: *I'll work hard when I think it matters, when it gives me a chance to shine. Otherwise, I'm saving my energy for the next big play.*

During one of the tryout sessions on a blistering August afternoon, McGraw half-stepped through a play because the runner had been stopped right at the line of scrimmage. As a linebacker, McGraw didn't think he needed to help with the tackle. So McGraw slowed the instant he heard the lineman's pads slam against the runner's.

From nowhere, Coach Wheeler suddenly appeared at McGraw's elbow, screaming at him as if his hair were on fire.

"What are you doing?" the coach yelled. McGraw would never forget how angry he sounded.

"The lineman made the stop," McGraw replied, a little uncertain.

"Until that ball carrier is down on the ground and you hear the ball whistled dead, I want you chasing the runner as if your life depends on it!" Coach Wheeler leaned forward until his face was only a few inches from McGraw's. "You got that? Every play! EV-ER-Y PLAY!"

For the next two weeks, Wheeler seemed to be at McGraw's side, or in his face, or screaming in his ear, at every moment of the long practices. At first McGraw was amused because he was so sure that he would be needed as a starting linebacker, regardless of how much the coach might or might not criticize him. After all, McGraw had seen his competition. He knew he was better than all but one of the senior linebackers.

Then one day, Wheeler called McGraw into his locker room office. The coach was welcoming and friendly. He invited McGraw to take a seat, offered him a bottle of water, and then put a question to his young player.

"Do you want to make varsity this year?" the coach asked. *Here comes my offer*, McGraw thought to himself before replying that he did. Then, to his surprise, Coach Wheeler explained exactly what it would take to land a coveted varsity spot. It had nothing to do with natural talent and everything to do with effort, focus, determination, and hard work.

When Wheeler was finished, he asked the somewhat-stunned McGraw if he had any questions. McGraw shook his head—the coach had been so clear that there was no room for misinterpretation.

Finally, Wheeler softened and told McGraw, "You have a lot of potential. You did well on junior varsity last year thanks to your size, speed, and natural talent. But now you're going to be playing with kids who are just as big, just as fast, and just as talented as you. And some of them will be almost three years older than you. I know you can compete with them, but you've got to work at it, and that starts with hustling—all out— on every play."

No one had ever explained things to McGraw like that before, and it changed his entire approach to football. McGraw's teammates started calling him Harry Hustle, and Coach Wheeler hardly ever had to yell at him again. During his senior year, when McGraw's father was pressuring him to go for a college football scholarship, Coach Wheeler spent over an hour on the phone with McGraw, helping him sort out what he really wanted from what his father *told* him to want. That conversation had directly impacted his decision to join the police force.

Drifting out of his reverie, McGraw wrote "fair" on the third line of the paper in front of him. Wheeler did not play favorites when it came to determining who would start, or who would get the most playing time. If you hustled and got results, you played. He'd bench one of his all-county players for slacking off just as fast as he'd bench a third-string substitute.

McGraw continued to sift through his memories of high school football, and soon "sportsmanship" went on the next line. McGraw remembered Wheeler going up to a kid who was trash-talking and asking if he'd say any of those things to his mother's face, which shut the player up almost immediately.

After a few more moments, McGraw put "respect" and "do the right thing" on the next two lines as another Coach Wheeler story occurred to him.

During McGraw's junior year, word reached Wheeler that one of the team's star players had shoved his girlfriend around at a party. Wheeler confronted the young man. At first the player tried to dismiss the story as a rumor, and when that didn't work, he tried to make light of it, as if it were no big deal.

Wheeler suspended the young man from the team, which put his college scholarship in jeopardy and enraged the player's parents. The girl hadn't pressed charges, they argued, so why was Wheeler sticking his nose where he didn't need to? Some of the other players on the team thought the same. At a team meeting, Wheeler stood on a chair and explained his actions in two sentences.

"How many people here learned, probably in kindergarten, that you shouldn't hit people?"

When it became obvious that it wasn't a rhetorical question, the players started raising their hands.

"Wrong then, wrong now," Wheeler stated. He stepped down off the chair and left the room.

McGraw smiled to himself and wrote "clear standards" in the Coach Wheeler column. After a few moments, though, the smile slipped off his face. He suspected that the second half of his assignment wouldn't be so easy to complete.

Well, might as well get it over with, McGraw thought as he picked up his pencil to write "Gus" at the top of the WORST column. Before he started forming the first letter, though, he thought better of it and left the name off. *No telling who might see these notes. And anyway, I'll know who I was talking about.*

The first thing that came to mind about Gus's poor leadership was that the lieutenant was often deliberately late to evening detail, every night. *Must be some kind of power thing for him*, McGraw thought. He wrote "inconsiderate, rude" at the top of the column. Lots of police supervisors he'd encountered had a no-nonsense way about them, but Gus was particularly tactless and uncaring. He never made any pretense of caring about his sergeants' lives outside the substation, even when a little knowledge of that kind would help the shift run better.

Gus also had a habit of talking about the district as if it were his. He was always saying "my officers, my cars, my district." At first it had sounded like he was taking responsibility, but soon McGraw had figured out that Gus was really trying to diminish everything his sergeants and officers accomplished. However, the tune changed quickly when a police officer screwed up. Gus couldn't distance himself fast enough. That officer suddenly became "one of McGraw's guys" or "one of Jenkins's bums."

That's typical of Gus, McGraw reflected. *Everything that goes well is to his credit, and everything that goes wrong is someone else's responsibility. He almost never sticks up for the people below him, and when he does, it's with ulterior motives, when it's good for Gus.*

He plays favorites, especially if one sergeant or police officer has access to someone with power.

McGraw had heard a story about how Gus had coddled one troubled police officer whom most squad members suspected of having a serious drug problem. The cop was married to a niece of a city council member, and that was all Gus needed to know. The young man had finally ended up leaving the force and going into rehab, but until that day, in Gus's eyes he could do no wrong.

McGraw added "unclear standards," "plays favorites," "inconsistent," "doesn't take care of the team," and "takes responsibility only for positive results" to the list. As soon as he finished the last word, his jaw cracked in a massive yawn. McGraw looked at his watch. It was past time for him to get home and get some sleep.

During his commute, McGraw was preoccupied with thoughts of how he might take his first step toward leading like Wheeler. He was getting close to home when he decided to do something Gus would never think of doing: He would act on Stanley's suggestion and get Williams trained for the patrol wagon.

Later that night, shortly before first watch detail, McGraw approached Ramsey with the news. "I'm going to put Williams in the wagon with Somers tonight," McGraw told him. "You've got your own squad car tonight. Stay busy; write some tickets around Grant and Walnut. Keep the traffic moving down there and keep an eye out for people peeing in public or causing trouble."

Ramsey looked suspicious. "Why am I off wagon?" he asked. "Did I do something wrong?"

"Just a change of pace," McGraw assured the other officer. "Besides, in the next few weeks, you're much more valuable patrolling Grant and Walnut than you are in the wagon. If I've got you and another big cop like Cooper down there, it helps me put a lid on drunk and disorderlies." Ramsey just nodded and walked away.

A few minutes later, Melody Williams had a similar reaction to the news. "What did I do wrong?" she asked McGraw, the worry clear in her voice.

McGraw smiled and said, "I want you to develop your skills. I thought you might be tired of writing tickets every night."

Williams smiled back and admitted that she was.

"Use this as a learning experience," McGraw continued. "We're too dependent on Ramsey and Somers for wagon work right now. If one of them got sick or transferred, I don't know what we'd do. So I'm asking Somers to train you in wagon operations and prisoner handling for the next few weeks."

"I'd like that," Williams said. It might have been McGraw's imagination, but he could have sworn that her shoulders were a little less slumped and that she was standing a little taller. "Thank you, sir."

That was the first time McGraw had heard anyone in Midtown East say the words "Thank you, sir." He had extended one of his officers a modicum of respect, and almost instantly, the respect had been returned. *Maybe*, McGraw thought, *this leadership stuff isn't so difficult after all.*

CHAPTER 13

The Rifle

Williams's first night on patrol wagon duty passed uneventfully. Feeling pleased with himself the next morning, McGraw made a detour on his way home. Soon, he was pulling into the parking lot of Martin's Guns on Prospect Boulevard, which he had done twice before in the past six weeks.

Ever since his promotion, McGraw had been thinking about purchasing a Smith & Wesson patrol rifle. Rifles were allowed under department regulations at the discretion of the officer, but each officer was responsible for selecting a model and paying for the weapon out-of-pocket.

As McGraw leveled the display model in the shop, he admired how beautifully it fit in his hands. The only thing that had prevented him from purchasing this rifle several weeks ago was Peggy's concern that the $1,200 price tag did not fit in the family budget. She was setting aside money each month for a new roof on their house, and that gave the McGraws very little wiggle room in their finances.

Peggy was a teacher, and she took care of balancing the household books with the same care and precision she devoted to grading papers. McGraw was happy to hand the task over to her. His own mother had handled the budget while he was growing up, so that particular division of labor seemed right to him.

More importantly, McGraw had no confidence in his own ability to keep track of what was coming in and what was going out, especially now that he was working a night shift. Peggy, however, sometimes got annoyed because she had to make all the budget decisions on her own.

"I don't like doing this all myself," she had told him one Saturday afternoon after he'd sat, mostly silent, while she explained her plan for saving money for the new roof they'd need within a year.

"I do other stuff by myself," McGraw had pointed out. He began to list his share of the household chores, which included some—like taking care of the cracked branch on the backyard oak tree—that he hadn't gotten around to doing yet. "Division of labor is more efficient, right?" he had finished.

"I just wish it felt more like a partnership," Peggy had told him with a sigh. "I don't mind doing the grunt work, but I feel bad deciding on my own what we can and can't afford."

That was the problem with the patrol rifle. Every time McGraw mentioned it to his wife, she would tell him they didn't have the money. But now, thanks to his promotion, he'd gotten a raise. He was making over $150 a week more than he used to, after taxes, and in McGraw's mind that solved the affordability issue. *The rifle should be paid off in about two months, with no impact on the family budget,* he told himself.

It was over in a couple of minutes: A quick swipe of the credit card and the bright black and red box was handed to him over the counter.

When McGraw arrived home, Peggy was getting ready for work. He walked in to their bedroom, beaming, and held up the box. "I got my patrol rifle!" he exclaimed. "And I figured out exactly how to pay for it!"

"You did?" she replied without a smile. "That's great. I'm very happy for you." Then she pushed past him, flicked on the bathroom lights, and started brushing her hair.

"I figured it all out," McGraw continued, feeling his exuberant mood begin to deflate. "We'll pay it off with eight weeks of the extra money from my raise."

"That's fine," Peggy stated, her tone of voice still flat and cold. "I'm sure it will be fine." McGraw tried to catch her eye in the mirror, but she looked down and focused on plugging her curling iron into the outlet.

"You're mad because I didn't consult you first," McGraw guessed. "Aren't you?"

"I'm annoyed," Peggy clarified as she wrapped a strand of hair around the iron. "I'm annoyed that the only time you do any budgeting or planning is when you're trying to figure out how to buy yourself a new toy. And I guess that's fine. You're entitled. But it doesn't make me feel very good."

McGraw figured he should remind Peggy that the rifle wasn't a toy or an indulgence. "These rifles are becoming very important," he began, shoving his hands into his pockets and leaning against the doorframe. "Cops say you can settle down a hostile crowd just by showing your patrol rifle. And with certain types of dangerous characters, it gets instant respect and compliance. So without ever firing it, it could save someone's life, maybe mine. That's why the department is allowing them."

The look on Peggy's face told him the gambit had failed. "Don't try to guilt me into feeling differently," she shot back. "This isn't about your rifle, Adam."

"It isn't?" he echoed, genuinely surprised.

"Of course it isn't." Peggy jerked another chunk of hair away from her head and clamped the curling iron around it. "This is about what we agreed. If you give me all the responsibility for doing the budget, then you can't go off making $1,200 spur-of-the-moment purchases. You want the privilege of spending the money and none of the responsibility for balancing the checkbook." She paused as she opened the curling iron and teased the spiral of hair with her fingers. "Don't you see that?"

McGraw was silent for a moment. "I thought this was different because it's about work, and about what I *need* at work."

"Fine," Peggy muttered as she continued to tweak her hair. "Just buy what you like and leave me to make everything work. And now, I'm not supposed to say anything because what you bought might save your life some day."

"I already told you, it's simple," McGraw countered, not ready to give up. "My raise will pay it off in eight weeks. And since it's a work expense, it's even tax deductible." He paused for moment, uncertain. "Isn't it?"

"You just made my point for me," Peggy said, giving her hair one last pat and unplugging the curling iron. "Enjoy your new gun. But don't expect me to be happy about how you did this. You treated me like your peon, like some hired bookkeeper. It's disrespectful and it hurts."

McGraw was ready for another round, hoping to smooth things over by talking about the practical matter of using his raise to pay down the credit card debt over the next few months. But Peggy didn't give him the satisfaction. She brushed past him once again, snagged her purse from where it was hanging on the doorknob, and left the bedroom.

From the foyer, Peggy called out, "I'm headed off to work!" McGraw winced as he heard the door slam. Hard.

CHAPTER 14

Marriage Counseling

The house felt cold and quiet after Peggy drove off. McGraw knew he should eat, exercise a bit, and then go to bed and get some rest. However, the argument with his wife, combined with the constant stress he felt on the new shift, had left him too troubled and tired to stick to his routine. He wandered through the empty house as he tried to sort out his thoughts.

For the first time, McGraw realized why so many veteran cops said that first watch can take a toll on your overall health and even the best marriages. He and Peggy were starved for time together. They no longer hired a babysitter and went out on Friday or Saturday nights because McGraw, as a new sergeant, had to work weekends. Most weekday mornings, Peggy was gone or scrambling to leave by the time he got home. To ensure that essential information was passed along, the two of them had begun leaving terse notes for each other on the refrigerator door, which was a poor method of communication.

Beyond the strain his shift was putting on his marriage, McGraw struggled to remember the last time he had gone on a good run or lifted weights. He also wasn't sure when he had last eaten a balanced meal. The only places open during his shift were a burger joint and an all-night convenience store.

Feeling morose, McGraw looked out the kitchen window at his backyard. It wasn't long before he noticed that Stanley was outside, sunning himself on the patio with his morning coffee. *Maybe Stanley won't mind if I talk to him*, McGraw thought. *I bet since he was in the Navy, he'll understand some of what I'm dealing with.* McGraw pulled on an old jacket and walked to the back fence to say hello. As he'd hoped, Stanley invited him over.

As soon as McGraw sat down, Stanley asked him what was wrong. Although McGraw generally thought of himself as having a good poker face, he figured that this particular morning his worry and frustration were clearly displayed. Without preamble, he told Stanley about his run-in with Peggy.

"Did you and your wife ever fight about money?" McGraw asked after he had recounted the morning's argument.

"We used to stress about money," Stanley answered. "Especially when the kids were young and there really wasn't enough to go around."

McGraw rubbed at a smudge on his pants. Stanley's answer hadn't exactly been an agreement. *Fights and stress aren't necessarily the same thing.* "I read somewhere that fights about money are one of the main reasons people get divorced," McGraw said, still looking down. When he felt Stanley looking at him, he added, "Not that Peggy and I are in any danger of splitting up. She's my best friend, and we hardly ever disagree. When we do, it really eats at me, and I know it eats at her, too."

"So what are you going to do to fix it?" Stanley asked, swiveling his head to look back out at the yard.

"I guess I should take the rifle back to the shop," McGraw replied, thinking out loud. "But that's not going to solve anything. I'm still going to need it, and she's still going to be mad."

"Taking the gun back won't make her happy because that's not what she wanted," Stanley said, sounding certain. "She doesn't want you to go without a patrol rifle. It sounds like she knows exactly why it's important to you." The older man shook his head as a fond look crossed his features. "She's a cop's wife, which in some ways is not so different from being a military man's wife. Peggy's probably more worried about your personal safety than you are. I know that's how Margaret was. It sounds to me like your wife wants you two to be on the same side because you both want the same things."

"But we don't want the same things," McGraw countered. "She wants the roof fixed before I get a patrol rifle, and I want the opposite."

Stanley chuckled. "Try to get your mind off your gun for a minute, okay?" he suggested, holding up a placating hand. "When I say you want the same things, I'm talking about respect, affection, a good home, an education for your daughter, that kind of stuff."

McGraw thought about that. "Yeah, sure. I mean, I guess so. We never really sat down and talked about it in those exact terms," he said.

"Well, most people never do," Stanley replied, leaning forward to set his empty coffee mug on a low wooden table. "This thing we're working on, to help you clarify your leadership philosophy, it can help in your personal life, too," he stated.

When McGraw didn't answer, the older man continued.

"Think about what Peggy wants out of your conversations about money."

Although his mind was tired and his thoughts were sluggish, McGraw made a sincere effort to do as Stanley had asked. "She wants to let me know where we stand financially," he answered. Then, thinking about his wife's other comments, he added, "And she wants me to be involved in the decisions."

"Why?" Stanley asked with an encouraging nod.

"Because she thinks…no, she really believes, that we have to be partners. Equal partners when it comes to big stuff."

Stanley nodded again. "Why does she care about managing the money?"

"So that we can accomplish our goals, I guess. Like you said, send our daughter to college, pay the mortgage."

"So security is part of this," Stanley commented. "And Peggy also wants you as a partner so that you don't resent the decisions she makes. Maybe also because she thinks that the two of you can make better decisions than she can alone." Suddenly, he grinned at the younger man. "A little consultation with her, and you could have had your rifle without a fight."

McGraw sat back in his chair as he considered how different he'd be feeling if he'd bought the rifle with Peggy's blessing. "So when you were in the Navy, did you moonlight as a marriage counselor?" he asked, only half-joking.

"Sort of. In all those years of dealing with sailors who had to spend long periods of time away from home, I probably heard every conceivable hard luck story."

"You got involved with people's personal lives?" McGraw asked. He was a little surprised. Most of the police officers he knew would be shocked, offended, confused, or all three if their superiors butted into their off-duty business.

"The military is more paternalistic than most civilian organizations," Stanley answered. "When we say 'take care of people,' we're really talking about the whole package, on-duty and off." He zipped his fleece coat up a little more to ward off the rising breeze. "Besides, if you take some twenty-one-year-old newlywed away from his wife, or away from her husband, it's going to have an effect on that sailor's work. Only an idiot would ignore that aspect of leadership."

Stanley paused, and his features arranged themselves into what McGraw was coming to know as his "teacher look." "Does the good leader on your list show any interest in people's lives?" he asked.

Luckily, McGraw had put his Best/Worst list in his pocket before leaving the substation that morning. He pulled the sheet of paper from his pocket, unfolded it, and looked at the entries under Coach Wheeler's name. "First thing on the list, in fact, is 'concern for people,'" he confirmed.

After handing the list to Stanley so the other man could look over it, McGraw told his neighbor a couple of stories about Coach Wheeler, including how the coach had handled McGraw's attitude problem when he first tried out for the varsity team.

"It doesn't sound like he was overly concerned about being buddies with the players," Stanley observed.

McGraw laughed. "No, he was more likely to kick you in the tail than he was to hold your hand."

"So he balanced concern and compassion with a drive to get the job done," Stanley summed up.

"Yeah, but it was more than that," McGraw replied. "He wanted to get the job done, and he was willing to teach us, to invest time in us so that we learned. And he even went further than that. I always felt he had a better handle on what I was capable of than I did. He could see potential on the other side of a lot of hard work. He not only pushed me through the work, but he also painted a picture for me, showed me what I could be like if I were willing to keep at it."

"That's a great description," Stanley said. "Let's go inside so you can write that down."

CHAPTER 15

Right and Wrong

Stanley led McGraw in through the kitchen, down the hall, and into his study. With its bookshelves and souvenirs from Stanley's years in the Navy, the room looked like a cross between a library and a museum.

"Here. Use these," Stanley said, handing McGraw a spiral-bound notebook and a pen. He motioned toward a chair, then sat across from the younger man.

Before he could forget, McGraw jotted down some notes based on what he had told Stanley about Coach Wheeler.

"Now, what about the worst leader you identified?" Stanley asked after McGraw stopped writing. "Does that person show any sign of genuine interest in others?"

"Not really. He's concerned with himself, with how he looks, with taking credit," McGraw explained. "And he certainly doesn't invest the time in learning about people, at least not the way Coach Wheeler did."

McGraw paused to unzip his jacket. It seemed that Stanley's wife Margaret had another thing in common with Peggy—

they both liked to keep their houses warm. "Anyway," McGraw continued, "the thing about Coach Wheeler was that he wasn't afraid to do what was right, or what he believed was right."

McGraw told Stanley the story about the player who had shoved his girlfriend and about Coach Wheeler's assessment: It was wrong in kindergarten; it was still wrong.

Stanley laughed out loud. "So he had a firm sense of right and wrong. Where do you suppose that came from?" Stanley asked. "Where does anyone get a sense of what's right?"

"Well, Coach Wheeler said he got it, or at least part of it, in kindergarten," McGraw replied. "I suppose we develop our sense of right and wrong from a combination of things: our home life, our schooling, our experiences, any religious education."

"What about in an organization?" Stanley prompted.

"I guess in an organization, a leader has to adopt the values of the organization and build from there," McGraw told him. "I imagine you had certain values that, if they weren't peculiar to the Navy, were at least common to Navy people, right?"

Stanley nodded. "Exactly. The Navy values are Honor, Courage, and Commitment. Sailors are expected to serve with honor, have the courage to do the right thing, and make a commitment to the Navy and their shipmates to accomplish the mission." He paused and propped his feet up on the low coffee table between himself and McGraw, then looked at the other man. "Does your department have clearly articulated values?"

"Not that I know of," McGraw admitted. "It says 'Protect and Serve' on the side of every patrol car, but I don't think anyone takes those words seriously. They just describe what cops do." He shrugged.

"Well, does the person on the 'worst' side of your paper have any values that are obvious, whether they're good or bad?"

"Hmmm...ahhh...I'm not really sure," McGraw said slowly. "When I think about how to describe his actions, I'd say he's just self-interested. But I'm not sure I could tell you what's important to him, other than power and control."

"That tells me a lot, actually," Stanley responded. If he suspected they were talking about Gus, he wasn't letting on. "It says something about you, too. About what you think is important in a leader."

"What do you mean?" McGraw frowned.

Stanley smoothed out McGraw's list and looked back over it. "A lot of what you wrote has to do with how the leader interacts with subordinates," Stanley said as he scanned the two columns. Then, he betrayed his suspicions as to who McGraw's worst leader was by saying, "There's some stuff here about the results the department achieves, but not much about protecting and serving the public. Any idea why that is? Why your thinking regarding this leader runs along those lines?"

McGraw considered a print of an aircraft carrier on the wall beside where he sat. The ship was backlit in yellow light, as if dusk were approaching, and two jets drew straight lines parallel to the surface of the ocean.

"I guess I believe that if the leader gets stuff right with the people who work for him, the other stuff will follow. Not automatically, but at least more naturally."

"In other words, you think that if you as a leader protect and serve your squad members, inside the organization, then you can expect that they'll go out and protect and serve the public?" Stanley asked.

"I'd sign onto that," McGraw replied, flicking a quick thumbs-up signal with both hands.

"All right," Stanley said, swinging his feet off the coffee table and leaning forward. "By the way, there's no single answer to this stuff. Much of it is a matter of your personal philosophy, your own take on how things work."

"Okay, now that's a problem for me," McGraw replied. "It sounds like, uh, moral relativity or relativism, whatever. That whole, 'What works for me is what's good, period' approach." He shook his head. "I don't know about that, Stanley. I mean, Saddam Hussein led by terrorizing and killing people. That was his take on how things should work in Iraq. So is it defensible if he were to say, 'That's just my leadership philosophy'?"

"No," Stanley answered. "Because your philosophy still has to stand up to a bunch of tests: Will people follow you? And is it consistent with your values and the values of the organization? Finally, is it ethical?"

McGraw's eyebrows drew inward. "There's a word you hear a lot," he commented. "The media goes on about ethics every time some CEO gets locked up for fraud or stock manipulation or insider trading. But I'm not sure I know exactly what it means."

Stanley leaned back and laced his fingers together across his stomach. "Well, do you believe some things are right and other things are wrong, period, no room for discussion?"

When McGraw didn't answer right away, Stanley continued, "What about pedophilia? Exploiting children in the sex industry? Right or wrong?"

"Wrong." McGraw didn't hesitate this time.

"Okay. So we've just established that you believe some things are absolutes," Stanley smiled. "We haven't drawn up an all-inclusive list yet, but we have something to start with. What you believe about right and wrong influences how you make decisions on a day-to-day basis. Moving from a very general rule—'stealing is wrong,' for instance—to a specific decision is called moral reasoning."

McGraw still wasn't convinced that he agreed with the idea of absolutes. "But people see things differently," he countered. "They don't have the same interpretation of the same events, or even the same words."

He ran his fingers through his short hair, trying to think of a good example. "Okay. Beating up suspects is wrong, but you should hear some cops laugh about it. They call it 'street justice.' Then the same cops would tell you they see true injustice in the courthouse, when crooks and killers beat the rap on legal technicalities."

"Everyone has a different point of view," Stanley agreed. "But on the other hand, just because someone can rationalize unlawful behavior doesn't mean we all should. Those cops may call it 'street justice,' but I promise you, they also know it's wrong."

Stanley was silent for a few seconds as he gazed out the window behind McGraw's head. "Some things are right; some things are wrong," he reiterated. "But it's okay to have a discussion about what those things are. It's a little like what your coach said about learning not to hit people in kindergarten. 'Wrong then, wrong now.'"

"I still don't know about making that kind of call," McGraw said, shaking his head. "One of these days, I know I'm going to see a beat-up kid in our holding cell, because one of my officers used excessive force and is afraid to bring him downtown for processing. And I'll have to decide at that point whether to make the call to Internal Affairs."

"I learned something very early in my career about leaders and the responsibility to make the call," Stanley said. His eyes took on a slightly unfocused look as he mentally traveled back through the decades. "I was a midshipman at the academy, and I was conducting a haircut inspection. So we had the company lined up, and I'm walking through the ranks, checking haircuts and uniforms, all that stuff. And my company officer, a Marine named Cipriotti, is sort of walking through the ranks nearby.

Stanley looked up at McGraw. "Cipriotti had been a Corporal in the Korean War. By the time I knew him, he was a Captain, assigned to the Academy to teach leadership."

McGraw nodded. He wasn't an expert on military rank, but Cipriotti's standing sounded impressive.

Stanley resumed his story, "So I go up to this one midshipman, and his hair looks a little long to me, so I ask him, 'Did you get a haircut this week?' And he says yes. I look at his hair for a while, and then I decide to let it slide.

"Later, Cipriotti comes up to me and says, 'Who the hell was running that inspection? Was it you or the guy in ranks?' And I said, 'I was, sir.' But it comes out like a question, like, 'I was? Sir?'"

Stanley laughed at himself and at the memory.

He continued, "Cipriotti asks me, 'So why did you ask him if he'd had a haircut? His hair was either in regulation or not. He doesn't make that call. *You do*. And if I can't get you to make a simple call like that—your hair is too long or your hair is okay—how am I going to trust you with a ship, or a company of Marines?'"

Stanley raised his eyebrows. "Get it?" he asked McGraw.

"I think so."

"You've been promoted in order to make the hard calls on behalf of your department and the public," Stanley explained. "You asked for that responsibility when you took the sergeant's test. If you didn't want to make those calls, you should have stayed a patrolman, though I don't think that was ever in the cards for you, was it?"

A half-smile crept onto McGraw's face. "No, it wasn't."

"Okay, enough hundred-year-old Navy stories," Stanley proclaimed, levering himself out of his chair and stretching his arms above his head. "It's time for you to write a short description of a good leader and a short description of a bad leader. Don't just describe the one person in each column, but broaden your thinking a little bit to include other good leaders you've known."

"More writing?" McGraw asked, wincing at the note of whining that had crept into his voice. Peggy was the writer in the house. She had helped McGraw with his papers all through his college courses, and when he graduated, one of his happiest thoughts at the ceremony was that he'd never have to write another essay as long as he lived.

Stanley read the disappointment on McGraw's face. "Just take twenty minutes, and do it right here," he suggested. "Keep it brief, and use very simple words. U.S. Grant had great advice on writing, and he finished near the bottom of his class at West Point. Grant used to say that you should write as if you were sending a telegram to a fool, and that every word of it would be paid for by a miser."

Stanley walked to the door of his study. "I'm going to go get another cup of coffee and leave you alone. Would you like some coffee, too, or something else to drink?"

"No, thanks. I'm okay," McGraw said.

After Stanley had disappeared, McGraw stared at the notebook in his lap and remembered a Mark Twain quote that Peggy had once repeated aloud to him while they were reading in bed:

"Writing is easy. All you do is stare at the blank page until beads of blood appear on your forehead."

CHAPTER 16

Clear and Concise

When Stanley came back into his office after twenty minutes had passed, McGraw still had a blank page in front of him. The older man took one look at the clean sheet of paper and observed, "Good thing you're not in the news business, writing under deadline."

"This has always been difficult for me," McGraw admitted.

"That's because writing is hard work!" Stanley exclaimed. He walked farther into the room and braced his arms on the back of the chair he'd sat in earlier. "Here's a trick that might help: Instead of thinking that what you put down has to be perfect, just consider that you have to put something down that may be, in some way, remotely connected to what you want at the end."

He lifted one hand and wafted it through the air in a sweeping motion. "Write anything that comes to mind. Then write the next thing, then the next. After you fill up a page, take a look at it from the beginning. Cross out the crappy stuff and keep the good stuff; then try to make the good stuff better."

"Okay, I'll give it a try," McGraw said. *That advice was actually pretty helpful—I'm always afraid I'll write the wrong thing,* he reflected.

With a smile, Stanley left again, and McGraw started writing:

> A good leader is someone who is concerned with his people as much as he is concerned with the results his organization achieves.

He paused and reread the sentence. *Hmmm…that ain't so bad.* McGraw continued to write:

> He tries to help his people find work that they're good at and that makes them happy within the organization. He tries to help them learn new things so they can move on to other jobs if they want to. A good leader remembers that people are not machine tools, that they have families and spouses and children and want more out of life than work.

> A good leader tries to maintain a cheerful, positive outlook, even when things get bad. A good leader has lots of energy and keeps up with the changes in his field. He respects other people and tries to figure out what the right thing to do is, for the public, the personnel, and the organization. A good leader

has a plan and sets the direction for the organization, and he gets the opinions of other people in the organization when he is coming up with that plan and the goals that go with it. He lets people know the standards, lets them know what's important to him and what he expects from them. He is up-front about what's important to him, and he is as good as his word.

This time, Stanley had given McGraw half an hour before returning, and McGraw was genuinely surprised when he realized how much time had passed. "I'm not a great writer," he admitted as he passed the notebook to Stanley. "It's difficult for me. So any suggestions you have, I'm ready to hear them."

"Okay," Stanley said. He took a pencil from his desk drawer, made some marks on the paper as he read through it, then handed it back to McGraw.

"Here you go," he said. "Writing 101. Clear and concise. Whenever you can cut a word without changing the meaning of the sentence, cut it."

McGraw scanned the paragraphs he had written, and saw that Stanley had followed his own advice:

A good leader is ~~someone who is~~ concerned with ~~his~~ people ~~as much as he is concerned with the~~ <u>and</u> results his organization achieves.

He ~~tries to~~ helps ~~his~~ people find work <u>they enjoy</u> ~~that they're good at and that makes them happy within the organization.~~ <u>and encourages them to learn new skills.</u> He ~~tries to help them learn new things so they can move on to other jobs if they want to. A good leader~~ remembers that people are not machine tools, that they ~~have families and spouses and children and~~ want more out of life than work.

~~A good leader tries to maintain~~ <u>He has</u> a cheerful, positive outlook, ~~even~~ <u>especially</u> when things get bad. ~~A good leader~~ has lots of energy and keeps up with the changes in his field. ~~He~~ respects ~~other~~ people and ~~tries to figure out what~~ <u>does</u> the right thing ~~to do is~~, for the public, the personnel, and the organization. ~~A good leader has a plan and~~ sets the direction for the organization, and ~~he gets the opinions of~~ <u>in-volves</u> others <u>in the process.</u> ~~people in the organization when he is coming up with that plan and the goals that go with it. He lets people know the~~ <u>sets</u> standards, lets <u>people</u> ~~them~~ know what's important ~~to him~~ and what he expects ~~from them~~. He is ~~up-front about what's important to him, and he is~~ as good as his word.

"Now, use that and rewrite it," Stanley instructed.

"Yes, sir," McGraw answered automatically, which made Stanley smile.

"The proper response would be 'Aye, aye.' Try to remember that." He winked and left the room once again.

McGraw felt good; he could see progress on the sheet in front of him. He tore out the page with his original description of a good leader, and using it as a guideline, began to lay out some bullet points. He made some further edits as he went:

A good leader:

- Respects people and does the right thing for the public, the employees, and the organization
- Is concerned with people AND results
- Is as good as his word
- Helps people find work they enjoy and encourages learning
- Remembers that people are not machines; they want more out of life than work
- Has a cheerful, positive outlook, especially in difficult situations
- Is energetic and keeps up with changes in the field
- Sets the direction for the organization and involves others in the planning
- Sets standards and lets people know what's important to him and what he expects from them

McGraw read back over what he had written. *That's actually a really good list, even though I wrote it!* he thought. *I wouldn't be surprised if I saw something like this in some kind of professional development material.*

Feeling pleased with himself, McGraw decided to go ahead and tackle the second part of Stanley's assignment: describe a bad leader. He went through the same writing process, but didn't need any step-by-step coaching this time.

A bad leader:

- Will lie or stretch the truth
- Puts his own interests first
- Promotes himself ahead of his people
- Is disrespectful
- Won't let me do my job
- Doesn't pull his share of the load

"Good," Stanley commented after he had returned and looked over McGraw's work. "I mean it!" He grinned. "See how much better your writing is now than it was an hour ago?"

McGraw laughed. "I guess I had a good teacher."

After indulging in another smile, Stanley returned to instructing. "Here's what I want you to do next," he told McGraw. "You can use this as a guide, although you shouldn't be limited by this, and examine your own leadership style. Which of these characteristics do you have, from either list? How important are they to you? Then I want you to pick the top four values, either stated or implied in what you've written about a good leader, and rewrite them as if you're explaining your intentions to someone else."

"What do you mean, exactly?" McGraw asked.

"For instance, if you make an honest assessment and find that, yeah, you really do treat people with respect, then you'd put 'respect for others' on your list of values," Stanley explained. "From those values we'll develop some ethical rules for you. Those are statements that often start with 'I will.'"

McGraw took notes as Stanley spoke. He could tell that he was getting close to understanding the points of his leader's compass.

CHAPTER 17

Narcotics and Vice

McGraw left for work that evening feeling fired up because of his conversations with Stanley. He parked his car and entered the substation looking forward to making an honest assessment of his leadership throughout the shift. He congratulated himself on his decision to put Williams in the wagon and felt excited about other personnel moves he might be able to make.

As soon as McGraw entered the main room, his thoughts were interrupted by loud, raucous laughter coming from one corner. A knot of cops was gathered around Jenkins's workstation. "What's going on?" McGraw asked.

Jenkins looked up. "Here's the man we've been waiting for!" he exclaimed, a grin splitting his face. "Get a load of this, McGraw."

With an uneasy feeling in the pit of his stomach, McGraw walked over to join the other officers. Jenkins's computer was opened to YouTube. The video on the screen showed a grainy image of a police officer sound asleep and snoring loudly behind the wheel of his squad car. The video's title was "Sleeping Beauty on Patrol, CCPD." And as the camera zoomed in, McGraw felt his heart skip a beat. The snoring cop was Hitchcock.

"Here it comes; this is priceless!" Jenkins yelled. Hitchcock's snoring reached its loudest point, a roaring crescendo of sawing logs. Then Hitchcock's face relaxed into a ridiculous, dreamy half-smile as he sunk deeper in slumber. Everyone except McGraw burst into laughter again, which attracted the attention of the man who had just entered the room: Gus.

"Turn that damn thing off," Gus yelled across the open space. Clearly, he knew what they were watching. "There's nothing funny about it. It's a reflection on all of you, and you should all be ashamed." He pointed at McGraw and motioned him toward his desk.

"Internal Affairs is looking for the kids who put that online," Gus said. "Do you know when that video was shot?"

McGraw shook his head. "First time I've seen it."

"You're lucky," Gus growled, "because it might have been shot before you came here. The good news is that Hitch is gone. Suspended with intention to dismiss. He can appeal the firing, but he's done." A note of satisfaction crept into Gus's voice. "We won't see him again."

"Does that mean I'm short an officer tonight?" McGraw asked. His concerns were a bit more immediate than Hitchcock's potential firing.

"No, they sent a rookie over to take his place," Gus explained, jerking his head in the direction of a young man standing by himself near the wall. "You should put him on parking tickets and get Williams to do something else."

McGraw didn't mention that he'd already made other plans for Williams that night.

"Gus, if I can change the subject, the big convention is this coming weekend, and I wondered if there was any news about what support we'll be getting. All those things we discussed." McGraw concentrated on keeping his voice calm and positive.

"Not happening." Gus glared across the desk. "As I told you before, you should plan on relying on your own resources."

McGraw's eyebrows rose. "They turned down your request for Narcotics and Vice Units?" he asked. "That's unbelievable."

"It's none of your damn business what I asked for and what was turned down," Gus said with a scowl. His voice was beginning to grow more strident, a signal that usually prompted McGraw to back off.

This time, though, McGraw decided to forge ahead regardless. "You said you'd ask Herman Duncan about porta-potties for Walnut and Grant," McGraw reminded the lieutenant, still striving to keep any trace of hostility out of his voice. "Any news there?"

"I never told you any such thing," Gus declared. The veins near his temples were standing out, but McGraw knew he couldn't let this issue drop without a fight. It was too important.

"When we discussed what to do about public urination, you said..."

Gus cut McGraw off mid-sentence. "I'm telling you I don't recall, McGraw. That means forget it."

McGraw allowed himself to sigh. "So what *are* we looking at for the weekend?"

Gus leaned forward, crossing his forearms on the desk. "I guess you won't shut up until I lay it out for you," he said, biting off each word. "You'll get two extra cops from Sector Four. Sectors One and Two will cover Pleasantville for each night. So on Friday and Saturday nights, you'll have a total of twelve officers under you, which you should concentrate around the convention center and around the Walnut and Grant area."

"Okay," McGraw replied. "Thank you, sir."

Gus seemed startled by McGraw's sudden formality and looked at him through narrowed eyes, trying to determine if he was being sarcastic.

"You're welcome, Sergeant," Gus finally said, his tone of voice noticeably softer.

McGraw rose and began to walk back across the main room. Before he'd gotten very far, Hardy fell into step beside him.

"You look like someone just shot your dog," Hardy observed. "Are you upset about Hitchcock?"

McGraw snorted. "Nothing like that," he assured the other officer. "I just found out that we've got nothing for the weekend. No Narcotics Unit. No Vice Unit. Not even a porta-potty to piss in. Just a few extra bodies and extra coverage for Pleasantville."

Hardy's eyebrows drew together. "Are you sure about this?" he asked.

"Gus just told me."

Hardy shook his head slowly. "I made some calls," he said. "I thought the word might have gone up the chain by now."

McGraw stopped walking as they neared the wall and pivoted to face Hardy. "What are you talking about?"

"Last week I told you that I'd make some calls about getting help for us," Hardy explained. "You never asked me about it again, and I had nothing to report. But basically, I called around to some friends in Narcotics and Vice to find out why Walnut and Grant were refused coverage this weekend. They said no one in either unit had received any requests from this substation."

McGraw was flabbergasted. "Gus never even asked?"

"Looks like the *chief* never asked," Hardy clarified. "It's way over Gus's head. The deputy commissioner for patrol and the deputy commissioner for special units are feuding. They're dragging their heels, not helping each other."

"That's nuts!" McGraw felt the beginnings of anger bubbling up. *Two deputy commissioners are mad at each other, and my colleagues and I are the ones who have to suffer for it?*

"That's typical," Hardy corrected him. "The special units are always getting jerked around by patrol, so the deputy commissioner there decided to push back." He sighed. "Anyway, despite all that, I was hoping that my information would make its way to the commissioner's office."

McGraw was impressed by Hardy's reach, though he didn't show it.

Hardy continued, "Grant and Walnut are too important this weekend to be a political football. It's the one part of the whole city where both of those units should be. I can't believe nothing's happened."

McGraw gave the other officer a humorless smile as he turned to go. "My thoughts exactly. But thank you for trying to help."

The night started out quiet. There were few calls, and for the first time that week, McGraw was able to play his patrol memory game: picturing the buildings around the next corner, and then testing himself to see how well he had remembered the scene. He was pleased that he was getting to know the sector very well.

Then, at 1:30 McGraw got an urgent call from Somers. "Sarge, we've had an accident with the wagon."

"Anyone hurt?" McGraw asked, his mind racing through the possibilities of what might have happened.

"One prisoner, in the back," Somers replied, his voice sounding sheepish. "He, uh, wasn't properly secured."

"Call an ambulance; I'll be right there."

Within a few minutes, McGraw arrived on the scene of the accident, but there wasn't very much to see. Apparently, Somers had been pulling out into traffic on Marsden just as a driver was steering into the right lane. The accident had been a fender bender and neither vehicle was disabled; in fact, damage was minor. But the shock of the collision had knocked an intoxicated prisoner off the bench in the back of the patrol wagon and into the steel interior wall, causing him to injure his neck. McGraw could see the man being loaded into an ambulance with a neck brace on.

"We each thought the other one had belted him in," Somers explained, glancing toward the paramedics. Williams remained silent. She looked stricken, and McGraw knew she was fearful she'd be blamed. He kept his gaze on Somers, though. Somers was in charge, and he knew the accident was his fault.

Somers had given McGraw the run-down on the wagon, but McGraw still walked around it to see what had happened for himself. The wagon was dented now, like a lot of police vehicles, but none of its lights had been knocked out. Fortunately, the vehicle was still in perfect operating condition. McGraw radioed for Ramsey and Cooper. They would take the wagon for the rest of the night, and he would take statements from Somers and Williams back at the substation.

Gus was waiting for McGraw when he returned. "What the hell was Williams doing in that wagon?" he demanded. "And what did I tell you about her? She's good for nothing but writing tickets."

"You also told me she should be put somewhere else tonight, so the rookie could write parking tickets," McGraw replied. "Somers was training her on the wagon, Somers was driving, and if the prisoner was injured, that was Somers's responsibility, too."

"Listen, McGraw, get it straight," Gus said, slamming his hand down on his desk. "I never told you to put Williams in the wagon."

McGraw remained silent. He'd never implied that Gus had recommended Williams be put on wagon duty. Gus was just covering his rear end again.

It took a few more minutes for Gus to wind down and dismiss McGraw. When he did, McGraw decided to head back out on patrol as soon as he had finished taking Somers's and Williams's statements. *Nothing good is going to happen if I stay here with Gus*, he thought. In the parking lot, Jenkins, who was getting out of his patrol car, accosted him.

"Congratulations on getting rid of Hitchcock!" Jenkins exclaimed. He held his hand up for a high five, which McGraw pretended not to see has he walked past. "Some of us think maybe that was you holding the camera," Jenkins continued. Two officers who were with him echoed his laughter.

Putting Hitchcock out of his mind once again, McGraw spent the rest of the shift mulling over what might have gone wrong with the wagon. Maybe this wasn't a one-time occurrence. Maybe Somers and Ramsey had gotten in the habit of not using safety belts with the prisoners. *Some prisoners are filthy and smell to high heaven*, McGraw reminded himself. *It makes sense that if you could avoid getting close to them, you might be tempted to put them in the wagon and drive to the substation without belting them in.*

Or maybe the answer was simpler—maybe Somers and Ramsey had been working the wagon together for so long that they'd just become careless. And then again, maybe it was just as

Somers said: He assumed Williams had belted the prisoner, and Williams had assumed Somers had done it.

The sun began to rise at about 6 a.m. as McGraw's shift came to a close. He drove past Grant and Walnut on his way back to the substation. *What's this area going to look like on Friday night?* he wondered. He hoped he could settle his spat with Peggy before then, because he really didn't want to take his patrol rifle back to the shop. He wanted to have it ready and in hand for the coming weekend.

When McGraw sat down at his desk to finish the evening's paperwork, he barely suppressed a groan as he saw Gus coming toward him yet again. *What does he want now?* Maybe there was news about the wagon crash and the injured prisoner.

But instead of a quick update, Gus said only, "Follow me." He led McGraw upstairs into the conference room. This was going to be bad.

"Morning orders just came through," Gus began. "I've got official notice from the commissioner's office that one Narcotics team and two Vice teams have been detailed to Walnut and Grant this weekend."

"That's great news, Gus." McGraw meant it. *I wonder if we can chalk this up to Hardy.*

"Great news, my ass," Gus retorted, looking disgusted. "Do you know anything about this? How did this happen?"

"You didn't make a request for those units?" McGraw tried to play dumb.

"That's not the question, Sergeant," Gus persisted. "I asked you if you know how this happened."

McGraw considered lying for just a moment, then thought better of it. He and Hardy had done nothing improper, and had broken no rules. He had nothing to hide.

"I talked to Hardy," McGraw explained. "He knew there might be a problem with getting those units, so he made some calls. But I don't know anything else."

"Hardy made some calls," Gus said in a mocking, sing-song voice. He stabbed his finger in McGraw's direction. "Did it ever occur to you that this is exactly why Officer Hardy got assigned to this rathole? By putting his nose where it doesn't belong?"

"He knew we were going to have a rough weekend and he thought he could help."

Gus exploded. "You think you're so smart with your college degree and certificate from that new supervisor's school the commissioner is so proud of! You and Hardy, both of you! You think you can go around me, go around the chief of this substation, go over our heads? Do you know what it looks like when the chief gets this order from the commissioner's office and I don't know anything about it?"

McGraw stayed silent.

"I look like a horse's ass!" Gus yelled, pushing himself out of his chair and stomping around the conference table to stand in front of McGraw. "I look like I'm letting the lunatics run the asylum down here. What were you thinking? Tell me. What were you thinking?"

McGraw leaned back in his chair in an attempt to put a little more distance between himself and the lieutenant, but he made sure to look the other man in the eye. "We just want to make the convention weekend a success," he explained. "We assumed that was the goal. Hardy told some people in Narcotics what we needed for the weekend, and I guess it made its way up the chain over there."

To McGraw's relief, Gus backed up a few steps. "That's why Hardy's never going to get anywhere in this department," he spat. "And that's why you're not going anywhere either. Who the heck do you think you are? You have only about nine years on the force; I have almost twenty years on it. You have *not* earned the right to ask for anything, or even be heard for that matter."

Gus began to stalk toward the door. "I told you this was political, and as long as you're one of my sergeants, you remember that politics is never any of your damn business. It's above your pay grade." With a final glare at McGraw, Gus wrenched open the door and yelled over his shoulder, "Know your place. And stay the hell away from anything above it!"

CHAPTER 18

Blind Spots

At 2:30 a.m. on Friday morning, McGraw and Hardy stopped at a diner to take their meal break together. The big convention weekend officially started in just a few hours, and they had spent the entire evening in the vicinity of Walnut and Grant. Much to McGraw's relief, the area was pleasantly subdued, even for a Thursday night crowd. There were already plenty of convention-eers in the area, conspicuous because of the nametags they wore on lanyards around their necks.

"Not one robbery report this evening," Hardy observed. "That's pretty good, with a big convention in town." He looked out the window at a small group of well-dressed men who were walking a bit unsteadily in the general direction of the hotels. "Why are they wearing those things around their necks? They make themselves look like targets."

"I think they put them on inside the convention center and then forget about them when they leave," answered McGraw. He rolled his eyes. "But you're right, the tags practically announce, 'Hi, I'm from out-of-town and carrying cash. Mug me!'"

Hardy took a sip of coffee while he read the menu. "I'm betting this will *not* be a typical weekend down here," he said. "Narcotics and Vice did a pretty thorough job putting everyone on notice yesterday and the day before."

"I heard about that," McGraw replied. He closed his own menu. "You really think it will work?"

"It's a strategic approach," Hardy explained. "If you go around to the problem areas, the hotspots, the nuisance bars, and let them know that we are doing zero tolerance this weekend, that the slightest infractions will be investigated and prosecuted fully, it puts a damper on a lot of potential nonsense." He shrugged as if to imply that the rest was obvious. "The bartenders are ready to stop serving guys who have had one too many. They tell their drug-dealing regulars to get lost for the weekend. The johns tell the hookers to stay home or just stay off the streets, to work more discreetly."

McGraw shook his head. "Too bad it couldn't work like this every weekend."

"Then we'd lose our effectiveness," Hardy put in. "In Narcotics, I began to get a feel for how cops and crooks are part of the same human system." He brought his palms together in a slow motion as though pushing against some type of invisible resistance, then let them spring outward again. "There's a push-and-pull to it. The bad guys know we don't have the will or the resources to do zero tolerance every night. But if we use the threat sparingly, so it remains credible when we issue it, then they'll take heed when we need them to, like this weekend."

McGraw nodded as he reflected on what Hardy had said. *It's not ideal, but using the threat of retribution sparingly does make sense.* "It looks like Herman Duncan took care of the homeless problem," he commented.

"I saw that in the paper," Hardy replied.

McGraw had seen the same article. The Chamber of Commerce had funded an outreach and treatment program run by a non-profit organization based in Sector Three. Homeless people had vanished from the streets around the convention center almost overnight.

Before either man could say more about the outreach program, their waitress appeared. Hardy and McGraw each ordered sandwiches. Neither one was very hungry.

"Have you heard anything about Hitchcock?" Hardy asked. He glanced at McGraw, then looked down and began to unroll the napkin holding his silverware.

"No," McGraw answered, then sighed. "I know he made his own bed—figuratively and literally—but I still feel bad for him."

"You dodged a bullet with that guy," Hardy stated, sounding certain. "Who knows how much trouble he could have gotten you into if he'd hung around."

McGraw shrugged. "I never got a chance to follow your advice and put him on ticket-writing," he said. "Maybe that would have kept him out of trouble."

Hardy paused, obviously hesitant to say what he was thinking. "You know, McGraw," he began, "you were treating him with favoritism, whether you can see it or not. Even if you didn't like Hitch, you treated him differently just because you knew him." Hardy looked up and met McGraw's gaze. "You told me about your talks with Stanley, about the need to give your officers some autonomy. With Hitch you gave way too much autonomy to the one guy least able to handle it."

"I've been thinking about that," McGraw said. "When he disappeared in the early mornings, I wanted to think he was working his hotel case. All along he was probably taking regular naps." He winced at his own naïveté.

Hardy paused again, reluctant to lecture his sergeant. After an encouraging nod from McGraw, he said, "That was obvious to everyone in the squad except you. That's something you can learn from this. We all saw what you couldn't see. That was because you didn't want to believe you were playing favorites. But you were."

The waitress arrived with their meal as Hardy finished speaking, which gave McGraw a few moments to think. *How could I have been so foolish as to take Hitch at his word?* McGraw found himself wondering now if Hitch's entire hotel story—the young woman, the tourist, the hotel security chief—could have been a lie, told so that Hitch could manipulate his new boss.

After thanking the waitress for their food, Hardy continued. "The thing is, until that day when you and Stanley had me in to talk with you, in the conference room, all I really knew about you was your lousy judgment with Hitchcock. I had you lumped in with Lurch, Jenkins, the whole clown parade running the substation."

"Yeah, but during detail each night I tried to show how I was different, that I wasn't like those guys at all." McGraw couldn't help feeling a little defensive.

"What you do when you're a leader speaks so much louder than anything you say." Hardy drained his cup of coffee.

McGraw let out a long breath. "I hear you," he said. "It's a little hard to take, but I'm glad you told me that."

"Everyone's got their blind spots," Hardy replied. Then, in between bites of his BLT, he told a story about being a rookie in Narcotics. A senior officer named Frank had taken him under his wing. Frank was the nicest guy in the world to Hardy. Showed him the ropes. Watched his back. Then one day Internal Affairs busted Frank. He'd been stealing Narcotics evidence and selling it on the side for years.

"I was scared to death that I'd get pinched, too," Hardy recalled. "I was so close to Frank that Internal Affairs had every right to assume I knew all about what Frank had been doing. So when I appeared for my interview, I tried really hard to convince them of my innocence. And, I'll never forget this. The investigator said to me, 'Relax, kid. We get it. You were clueless. In fact, we figure that Frank never even tried to bring you in on his racket because you're just too damn dumb!'"

They both laughed so hard that heads turned in the diner.

"I owe you a big apology, Hardy," McGraw said, reaching across the table for the ketchup bottle. "I steered clear of you for weeks, partly because you were a marked man, but really because I was threatened." He squirted a generous helping onto his fries. "I thought I could control Hitch, which was wrong, but I also knew I couldn't control you. From the start, I was acting more like Gus than I could even admit. It was all about control."

"That's how the culture in this department can work on you," Hardy agreed. "If you're not careful, you can start imitating the guy above you, even if he's the last guy you'd want to be. It's pretty frightening."

McGraw changed the subject. "So what's your advice on how I handled Williams and Somers with the wagon?" He was intent on using Hardy as his sounding board in developing the squad.

"My opinion?" Hardy asked. He followed McGraw's lead and squeezed some ketchup onto his own fries while he thought. "Somers probably didn't train Williams properly about safety belts in particular and prisoner handling in general. It's a lucky thing for everyone that the prisoner wasn't badly hurt."

"I still think it was right to put Williams on the wagon," McGraw said. "I want to start stretching the people here, to give them a chance to prove they're not what Hitch said they were, residents of Screw-up City."

Hardy shook his head. "You want to stretch them, but don't forget that they're here in first watch Sector Three because they're not the sharpest knives in the drawer." He popped the last bite of BLT into his mouth, then said, "Somers probably needed a little more direction in how to train a fellow officer. I think you left too much to chance there. Stretch them, but not to the point where they break."

McGraw knew that all of Hardy's comments were right on the mark, but it was still painful to sit through the other officer's even-handed critique. He dipped the tips of his fingers in his water glass and pressed them onto the corners of his eyes.

"Well, at least Stanley and I will have a lot to talk about," he said with a rueful grin.

CHAPTER 19

The Breakfast Club Reconvenes

McGraw and Stanley met over breakfast the Monday after the convention.

"Thanks for coming out here again," McGraw said as they were seated at the Windsor. "I've been thinking—would you want to talk to the police department's human resources division about doing some consulting work? Every sergeant needs to get the kind of training you're giving me, Stanley."

"No, thanks," Stanley said with a good-natured smile. "A consultant is someone who comes in, looks at your watch, and tells you what time it is." He tapped himself on the chest. "I like to think of myself as just a teacher. But you can keep buying me these great breakfasts for as long as you want."

"I don't have my homework," McGraw admitted after they'd ordered. "I know you asked me to do a self-analysis of my own leadership, but it's been tough." Trying to ignore the sense that he was once again an elementary-school student who had disappointed a favorite teacher, McGraw forged ahead and filled his neighbor in on the details of the previous week.

"Bottom line, I just about got burned—badly—for putting Williams on the wagon," McGraw finished. "No disrespect, but your idea about developing people by giving them tasks that are just beyond their reach doesn't look so hot anymore."

Stanley raised his eyebrows. "Well, if you were expecting it to be without risk, I guess it does look like a bad idea," he agreed. "But I did tell you that when you let people stretch a bit, they're going to fail sometimes."

McGraw looked out the restaurant's plate-glass window. At this hour, a steady stream of commuters were making their way to work. "This 'failure' could have been really expensive," he noted as he watched a cab pull over to the curb. "The guy in the back of the wagon could have been paralyzed or killed. And I still don't know who's really at fault, whether it was Somers or Williams who neglected to belt the guy in. I guess it was Somers, because he was in charge."

Stanley followed McGraw's gaze out the window, but he addressed the subject at hand. "So, the lesson here is this: Your job as a leader is to set people up so that they succeed while also building a safety net so that when they do fail—and they will at some point—it isn't deadly to the mission or the organization."

McGraw nodded. *Easier said than done*, he thought.

"That failure can be a wonderful teaching moment for Williams," Stanley continued. "When I fail at something, I'm forced to realize what I don't know. And that can make me more likely to listen to other ideas—and to learn." He shifted in his chair, facing the table once more. McGraw followed suit, and Stanley caught his eye.

"If I'm on your team, your job, as my leader, is to make sure that you set up the situation so that my failure isn't catastrophic," he explained. "That's why experienced surgeons oversee procedures when new surgeons are learning. Something goes wrong, the old hand is right there."

McGraw thought back on his time as a sergeant. "So far I've probably gone to one extreme or the other," he reflected. "I was either a micromanager, or I stepped away completely. Now it seems like the answer is in the middle."

"The answer is often in the middle," Stanley chuckled, leaning back so that the waiter could place a steaming omelet in front of him. "When you have someone like Williams, who doesn't have a ton of experience, you're going to stay a little closer. Someone like Hardy doesn't need to be watched that closely."

McGraw sniffed in appreciation as the scent of sausage links and pancakes wafted up from his own plate. "Speaking of Hardy, I almost hate to admit it, but he really helped pull us through the convention. He stuck his neck out, made some calls, and really saved our bacon."

Stanley didn't look surprised. He glanced up from cutting his omelet. "Hardy's more of a pro than you've been giving him credit for. And he's probably embarrassed about the way he treated you at first, with all those snotty remarks. He knows that wasn't him at his best."

McGraw nodded his head. "Even though Gus was angry at both of us, I could tell that in the end he was glad the convention weekend went well. Herman Duncan sent him a big basket of fruit in gratitude, and guess what Gus did? He locked it in his office and took it home with him in the morning."

Stanley snorted. "So he took all of the credit for what you and Hardy did."

"Yeah," McGraw confirmed. He stabbed a chunk of pancake with his fork and dragged it through a pool of syrup for good measure. "And he blamed us for the way we got it done. That's Gus."

"You're not like that at all, are you?" Stanley asked. "You don't shift the blame and grab the credit."

McGraw sensed a trap, but stepped in it anyway. "Of course not." It might have been his imagination, but he was sure a mischievous gleam had just appeared in the other man's eyes.

"Tell me again whose fault it was that the prisoner got injured," Stanley prompted.

"I just told you it was basically Somers's fault," McGraw responded immediately. "Even if Williams neglected to belt in the prisoner, Somers was at fault because he was in charge."

Stanley persisted. "*Who* was in charge that night? Refresh my memory."

McGraw suppressed a sigh. *I think I see where this is going.* "I was in charge," McGraw amended. "I assigned Williams, I told Somers to train her, and the injury to the prisoner was my fault."

Stanley finished chewing a bite of pineapple from the fruit cup that had accompanied his omelet, then asked, "Did you say as much to your squad? To Williams? To Somers?"

McGraw looked down. "No."

"Well, that should be part of your debrief after the smoke clears on this."

"Debrief?" McGraw had heard the term before and knew what it meant, but it wasn't something the police force used officially.

"A debrief, an after-action review," Stanley explained. "Some people in the military call it a 'hot wash.' You pull everyone together and figure out what happened and why. Most important, you figure out how you can make sure it doesn't happen again. This experience is valuable, after all, only if you guys learn from it."

McGraw was dubious. "I don't know," he said as he sliced a sausage link into bite-sized pieces. "You get cops together for meetings like that and they just turn into shooting galleries. Everyone just complains and points fingers of blame."

"Depends on how you set it up," Stanley replied. "Most important, it depends on how you, the boss, react to criticism. You set the ground rules: no personal attacks, keep focused on actions, that kind of thing."

Stanley gestured toward himself with his coffee cup before taking a sip. "In other words, I don't get up and say, 'This whole thing was McGraw's fault because he's an idiot.' I say, 'This all started with McGraw's failure to'...what?" Stanley asked.

"McGraw's failure to spell out the training," McGraw finished.

Stanley smiled and nodded, then raised his mug in a toast. McGraw lifted his water glass.

"Here's to your willingness to confront all this stuff and try to learn from it," Stanley declared. "A leader has to be able to admit he doesn't know everything."

"Thanks," McGraw said as they clinked their glasses together. "I guess I'm willing to confront my ignorance."

"Puts you way ahead of the pack," Stanley said, then winked. "Cheers!"

PART FOUR

CHAPTER 20

Honest Assessments

A few days after his breakfast with Stanley, McGraw came in to the substation early. He headed straight for the conference room and spent a half-hour analyzing his behavior and performance, using his description of a good leader as a guide.

"Let's see," he muttered, looking over the list of attributes, "a good leader..." he trailed off as he read each bullet.

- Respects people and does the right thing for the public, the employees, and the organization
- Is concerned with people AND results
- Is as good as his word

McGraw frowned. *Okay, I guess I'm going to have to give myself a minimum pass on those things,* he thought. He hadn't *not* done any of them...but on the other hand, there was a lot of room for improvement.

Then he got to:

• Helps people find work they enjoy and encourages
  learning

"Not so much on that one, I'm afraid," McGraw admitted. He put an F next to that line, then forced himself to think through how he had dropped the ball. *I micromanaged Williams's ticket-writing and didn't invest any effort in finding out what talents she might have. I also told myself I was giving Hitchcock a chance to develop, but in that case, I was giving too much latitude to a bad officer whom I knew required closer supervision.*

Then there was Hardy. *Hardy was a potential asset to me from day one, but I allowed his attitude to prevent me from seeing the value he could bring to the squad.*

Almost immediately, McGraw laughed at the thought, then forced himself to recognize something closer to the truth: He had been intimidated by Hardy's experience. Hardy was his equal. The two men probably would have made sergeant together if Hardy hadn't had his run-in with his former chief. *Hardy might someday prove to be a better sergeant than me,* McGraw thought. *He really might be even better suited for leadership than I am.*

McGraw knew he had let all those thoughts bother him, to the point of interfering with his work. He was glad his attitude toward Hardy had changed, and that he was now able to use the other officer's talents and abilities constructively.

McGraw looked a bit further down the list.

- Has a cheerful, positive outlook, especially in difficult situations

I've done all right during most of the bumps along the way...but I think maybe I take my head-to-heads with Gus a little too hard, McGraw mused. Hardy had commented several times on what he called McGraw's "someone-shot-my-dog" look. He'd have to work on that.

McGraw gave himself a C on his attitude. *Again, could be worse...but there's also a lot of room to improve.* Next, he read:

- Is energetic and keeps up with changes in the field

"I've got to get out in front on this one," McGraw said to himself, drawing a star on that line.

Now that the convention was behind him, McGraw wanted to take a step back and determine what he really wanted to accomplish in Sector Three. So far the job had involved any number of small, intense distractions, which was natural in patrol—but they had kept him from moving forward at the pace he'd wanted to.

Before making sergeant, McGraw had somehow developed the idea that work was all about action, about doing something. Maybe it was all that time on the football field. Playing defense, especially linebacker, meant you were in on, or trying to get in on, every play, every tackle. It was about pursuit, about constant motion. And when he had slowed down, Coach Wheeler had been on his case.

Now McGraw was coming to the late realization that leadership doesn't always call for the same frenetic motion. *Perhaps I need more time to think and get to know my squad.* The thought wasn't nearly as frustrating as it once would have been.

The last line on the paper read:

- Sets standards and lets people know what's important to him and what he expects from them

McGraw put an F next to that item, then flipped to the next blank page in his notebook. It was time to tackle his next assignment: identifying his own top values.

Stanley had told McGraw to look for patterns—ones he approved of as well as ones that upset him—in order to hone in on what his personal values were. First, McGraw wrote "Respect" at the top of the next page. He'd already known that it was important to him. Then, considering that much of what had gone wrong within the squad could be traced back to the fact that he hadn't communicated very well, he put "Communication" on the next line.

Doodling a formless squiggle on the margin of the page, McGraw thought about why he'd made Coach Wheeler his exemplar for a good leader. He kept coming back to the story about Wheeler confronting the team, some parents, and even some of the other coaches after he'd benched the star player for pushing his girlfriend. *That, more than anything else, is why I admire Wheeler*, he decided.

With that thought, "Moral Courage" went on the page underneath "Communication." McGraw knew all about physical courage—tangling with three-hundred-pound offensive linemen and two-hundred-forty-pound fullbacks had taught him a great deal about fortitude. But when it came to having the guts to do the right thing, the unpleasant thing, the distasteful thing, he wasn't convinced he was in Coach Wheeler's league.

Thinking about Wheeler also reminded McGraw of his exemplar for worst leader: Gus. *The thing that bothers me most about Gus is that he'll say one thing to your face, then do or say something completely different when it suits him.* McGraw wrote "Character" on the list of values.

Stanley had told McGraw to explain these values in writing, as if in a letter to another person. McGraw carried the list with him and worked on it in his spare moments over the next week. On the evening before his next breakfast meeting with Stanley, he showed his list to Peggy, who was reading in bed as he was getting ready for his shift:

> Respect: A leader treats people with respect, listens to their ideas, and is helpful.

Communication: A leader lets people know what he wants. He is clear about the organization's goals, about his personal idiosyncrasies, and in his evaluation of performance, both his own and others'.

Moral Courage: A leader does the right thing, regardless of the consequences, even when it's unpleasant.

Character: A leader acts in a way that will make others proud to be associated with him. Actions are more important than words; words and actions must be consistent.

"What do you think?" McGraw asked after Peggy finished reading the page and set it down on her nightstand.

She was silent for a moment, then commented, "I think all this stuff can help us, too."

McGraw grinned. "That's what Stanley said."

"That argument we had about your rifle," Peggy began. She wove the hem of the sheet between her fingers as she gathered her thoughts. "I think we could have avoided that if we'd both been more clear about what we wanted."

"You want to feel like I'm your partner in the financial decisions, right?" McGraw asked. This time, he didn't want to take any chances and assume he knew what Peggy was thinking.

"Yeah," Peggy said, smiling. "I think so."

"And…let me try this while I'm on a roll…you place a higher priority on being able to sleep at night, without worrying about money." McGraw crossed the room and sat on the edge of the mattress.

"Yes, but I also want you to have the things you need to do your job. Being a police officer is dangerous, and the patrol rifle is not a toy. Like you said, it could actually save someone's life. Maybe yours." McGraw could tell from the look on his wife's face that she meant what she'd said.

"What about hot buttons?" McGraw asked. "In this description of communication, when I wrote, 'A leader lets people know about his idiosyncrasies,' I was talking about things that get under your skin, that I might not know about, or I might know but choose to ignore."

"Give me an example," Peggy prompted. She reached out and took his hand, giving it an encouraging squeeze. "I promise not to get defensive."

"Something you do that bugs me?" McGraw replied. "Okay, when we're out with people and someone makes the predictable cop joke, you know, 'Don't arrest me!' and silly stuff like that, you usually laugh right along with the other folks."

A look of surprise crossed Peggy's face, and then she met his eyes, clearly contrite.

"I'm sorry," she said, flipping the sheet off and scooting up on the mattress so that she could lay her cheek on McGraw's shoulder. "I…you're right. I should be more sensitive."

"Yeah, that's it," McGraw laughed, putting his arm around her and squeezing her closer. "Like me. Mr. Sensitive."

Peggy laughed too, then sat back. "Okay," she began. "My hot button? It's not about money. It's you using your safety as the trump card to win arguments."

"What do you mean?" McGraw asked, frowning. He was genuinely puzzled.

"Well, when your back was against the wall in that argument about the rifle, all you had to do was say you were sorry for not thinking about me," Peggy replied. She looked at him, her eyebrows raised. "Do you realize that? That's all I wanted to hear. I wanted you to acknowledge that you should have talked to me before buying the gun."

McGraw nodded, taking in what his wife was saying.

"And you didn't do that," she continued. "You went the other way. You started in about how the rifle might save your life, which is true." Peggy held up a finger. "But it was also unfair and off the point. It's like you were accusing me of not caring about your safety, just because I was bringing up the subject!"

"So first I ignored you," McGraw said, recapping what he had heard. "And then I tried to say you shouldn't care, since I ignored you for something I need for my safety."

Peggy nodded. "That was really underhanded," she told him, reaching up to push away a strand of hair that had fallen into her eyes. "And it's not the first time you've done it. Whenever you're about to lose an argument, you find a way to make it all about your physical safety on the job, just so I can't win."

Although McGraw's instinctive response was to feel defensive, he knew that his wife had a point. "Wow," he said. "I never realized that. I'm really sorry."

"Don't worry about it," she replied, grabbing him around the neck and planting a kiss on his cheek. "Stanley and I will have you whipped into shape in no time."

CHAPTER 21

Stanley's Policy

The next morning, McGraw and Stanley enjoyed another breakfast at the Windsor. When they had nearly cleaned their plates, McGraw took out his list of top personal values and passed it across the table. Stanley took his time looking over the other man's work, and finally pronounced it sound.

"I don't know that I've ever spent this much time thinking about my approach to leadership, or to my relationships, for that matter," McGraw shared. "Knowing where I'm coming from helps me figure out where I should be headed. It's like having that compass you mentioned a while back."

"Good," Stanley said. "You know, that compass analogy really is accurate. You can imagine lots of similarities between a ship without a compass and a floundering supervisor." He reached across the table and handed the list back to McGraw. "This is going to help you get focused. It's also going to help the people who work for you, because you're eventually going to share this with them when you're finished."

McGraw's eyebrows shot up, and he felt a stab of unease in his gut. "I am?"

"Sure," Stanley replied, grinning at McGraw's disappointment. "Remember I said you've got to let other people see this? One of the big benefits of developing a leadership philosophy is that you can let people know where you stand and what's important to you."

McGraw grunted an unenthusiastic assent.

"Just think about how much time people spend trying to figure out what the boss wants," Stanley continued. "Think of the projects that have to be redone, or the priorities reset. Think of the confusion when people can't make sense of one of your decisions." He pointed to the list in McGraw's hand. "If they have this, they can figure out why you're doing what you're doing. And they can hold you to it."

"Is that always a good idea?" McGraw asked, still feeling dubious. His mind was filled with a vision of everyone in his squad bombarding him with the details of how, exactly, he was failing to live out his values.

"Suppose you say, in your philosophy, that you want people to be scrupulously honest, and so they should expect the same from you," Stanley suggested. "You tell them that if you have any doubts, you'll ask for an explanation. And you also tell them to ask you what's going on if something looks fishy to them."

"That's what I'm going to do?" McGraw asked.

Stanley drained the last sip of coffee from his mug and nodded. "Consider the possibilities. In one scenario, every once in a while you have to explain a decision to someone who has a question about your actions. On the other hand, if you've never told them, explicitly, that honesty is important and that it's okay for them to ask you about things, if they do see something that doesn't look right, they're not going to ask for an explanation, and they'll just go around assuming the worst."

"I see your point," McGraw replied. *That actually sounds a lot like what's happening throughout the substation now.*

Stanley leaned forward and laced his fingers together. "I know that this might be a little scary if you're not used to operating this way. You're going to come right out and say: This is what I believe, and these are the standards. And by sharing them, you're inviting people to hold you to them. That's a higher standard of performance than just assuming everyone knows what you want."

Stanley paused as he held out his mug to be refilled by a passing waiter, then continued, "The alternative to sharing your standards and expectations is being a boss who doesn't say what the rules are precisely because he wants to change them all the time."

That's Gus up one side and down the other, McGraw thought. Aloud, he said, "That's how you get a roomful of cynical, disgruntled cops."

"Especially in tough times," Stanley agreed. "Or in high-stress occupations, like the police, where there's always a crisis somewhere. Under stress, under pressure, which is always in the police department, people respond to a leader with character. It's the only thing they can count on."

He pointed at McGraw. "If I follow you because I think you have my best interests in mind and because I'm proud of the association with you, then I'm not going to jump ship at the first sign that things are going wrong. Hang on." Stanley twisted around in his seat and reached into the pocket of his jacket, which was hanging on the chair's back.

"Here, read this," he instructed as he slid a piece of paper across the table to McGraw. The heading read: "DEPART-MENT OF THE NAVY."

From: Commanding Officer, USS *Nevada* (SSBN 733) (Blue)

To: All Hands

Subj: Command Policy

1. My command policy is developed from my expe-rience and personal philosophy. Your knowledge and observance of these principles will help en-sure that USS *Nevada* (Blue) is always ready to perform its mission and that our ship is a safe and reasonable place to work and live.

2. Ideas and ideals to which I subscribe:

a. Nevada's *mission is threefold*:
   - To keep the peace through the highest state of strategic readiness
   - To maintain the ability to fight and win any conventional encounter
   - To provide each man on board the opportunity for personal and professional success

b. *Believe in yourself.* Seek and accept responsibility, both as a leader and as a follower. Act as if the success of the ship depends on your actions alone.

c. *Believe in your job.* We don't get paid enough for the hours, the effort, or the dedication it takes to do our jobs, so there has to be something else we value. Take pride in the fact that your nation depends on you to protect its citizens.

d. *Try to be the best.* You won't always reach your most ambitious goals, but you'll be far ahead of where you'd be if you planned for mediocrity.

e. *A good leader works to make each follower a success.* This sometimes requires both leading and pushing.

f. *The Navy is only as good as its people.* I am personally interested in each of you, your family, and your success. Let the command know about your problems. Seek help.

g. *Be a good shipmate.* The sea is a demanding mistress, and we must watch out for each other.

h. *Be proud of your ship.* Show visitors and inspectors how good we are.

i. *Be honest in all you do.* If I can't trust you, I won't keep you on board.

j. *Provide forceful backup to your seniors.* Nobody is infallible. If the ship or someone is headed into danger, take action to bring the danger to light.

k. *Provide steady support to your juniors.* They look to you and your experience to show them the way.

l. *Keep high standards.* If you ignore a situation that needs correcting, you have just established that as your standard.

m. *Punishment should not be the first step in correcting minor errors.* Counseling and instruction are a more constructive approach.

n. *Maintain a healthy skepticism.* "Know" rather than "assume." "Expect" a job to be done right, but "inspect" to make sure it is.

o. *Maintain a "fix it now" attitude.* Take time to plan and perform a job right the first time. If you are asked to do the impossible, register your concern. If told to try anyway, give it your best effort.

p. *Be part of the solution, not part of the problem.* Don't just identify problems; propose solutions.

q. *"Practice daily with the guns."* We must practice daily in order to be able to fight.

r. *Learn to play hurt.* We must be able to continue fighting while combating battle damage.

s. *Training is key.* The crew must know how to operate the ship in day-to-day and emergency conditions.

t. *Give priority to the ship's objectives.* All planning must begin with the overall goals of the ship. It does us no good to have departments reach goals if the ship fails.

u. *Illegal drugs have no place in the Navy.* Alcohol abusers need help as a first step.

3. I will follow these principles with few exceptions. Consider their meaning and apply them to how you do your own job.

S. R. Sabato, Commanding Officer

CHAPTER 22

The Marker

"The USS *Nevada*…what kind of ship is it?" McGraw asked Stanley as he scanned back through the other man's command policy.

"The *Nevada* is a nuclear submarine," Stanley answered, sounding as casual as he would have if he'd been telling McGraw that it was raining outside.

McGraw's eyes snapped up in surprise. "You commanded a nuclear sub?" he echoed.

"Yep," Stanley replied, pride entering his voice. "One of the greatest jobs ever."

McGraw held up Stanley's memo. "This is pretty thorough." He felt intimidated.

"By the time I wrote that," Stanley explained, "I'd already been in the Navy nineteen years. I had a chance to see lots of skippers—both good and bad—and watch a lot of leaders."

McGraw nodded, feeling a little better about his own relative lack of experience. "Did you ever think twice about distributing this?" He looked back down at the memo. "I mean, I can imagine some people using it to sharpshoot every little thing you did."

When Stanley didn't answer, McGraw looked up. The older man was studying him, the hint of a smile on his face.

McGraw held up his free hand in mock surrender. "Okay, what I mean to say is that's what *I'm* afraid of," he clarified. "Some of my squad members would love to use this as a checklist for taking potshots at the boss. It could undermine my authority with them if, let's say Hardy and I are at odds over something, and suddenly he goes around saying, 'Respect? Respect? Where's the new freakin' incident forms?'"

"Well, that's always a possibility," Stanley acknowledged. "But keep in mind that this isn't a written promise that everything you do is going to be perfect. It's a plan."

McGraw opened his mouth to respond, but Stanley held up his index finger to silence him.

"And," Stanley continued, "if you really think about it, the boss who should be most worried about publishing something like this is the boss who doesn't believe in it and has no intention of following it. It's the boss who is a shady character to begin with."

McGraw stared into the bottom of his nearly empty coffee mug for a few moments. "Got it," he said eventually. "If I want my whole squad to step up and start being accountable, then I've got to start by having the guts to put this out there and be held accountable for it."

"If you're going to raise the stakes, you've got to put something into the pot," Stanley stated with a shrug. "This is your marker. It's an IOU to everyone, in black and white, that you're accountable to them, which is why you expect them to be accountable to you, to each other, to the public and to the department."

McGraw continued to look over Stanley's statement. "Can I start writing my own statement by adapting your version?" he asked.

Stanley smiled. "Borrow from mine; borrow from anyone else's you can get hold of," he told McGraw, gesturing at the window as though to include the entire city. "There are no points for originality. What you write only needs to be true to what you believe and want to accomplish."

McGraw returned home and slept better than he had in weeks, eventually waking up at 5 p.m. *Maybe I'm finally adapting to working nights.* He spent much of the evening prior to his shift working on his leadership philosophy. His first attempt was clumsy and repetitive, but after a few more rounds of edits using Stanley's "cut everything that doesn't need to be there" strategy, McGraw felt he had at least produced some raw material to work with.

Just as Stanley had advised him, McGraw set the document aside for a week, and when he returned to it, he discovered it wasn't as bad as he'd recalled. He spent some time trimming it down, then, a few days later, took one more hour to make some additional changes.

When McGraw was finally able to read through his personal leadership philosophy and feel that it was ready, he called Margaret, Stanley's wife, and asked about Stanley's favorite restaurant. He looked up the name she'd given him, called the phone number listed, and made reservations for the following Sunday evening.

When she heard where they were going, Peggy insisted that McGraw dress up. He had grumbled about it, but when Stanley came out of his house in a blazer and tie, McGraw was glad Peggy had set a high standard for the dress code. McGraw drove the four of them to Sasso's, and after their wine glasses were filled, he proposed a toast.

"Here's to my mentor, Stanley," McGraw said, looking across the table at his neighbor. "You were generous with your time and experience at a time when I needed exactly what you had to offer. I thank you, and I'm pretty sure my team will thank you for what you taught me about being a better leader."

Stanley, uncharacteristically, had nothing to say. Later, Peggy would insist that the old sailor had been a little choked up. After the toast, McGraw pulled an envelope from his pocket and gave it to Stanley.

"Is this a bribe?" the older man asked. He opened the envelope and read McGraw's two-page leadership philosophy.

"This is wonderful," he said simply. McGraw felt happier than he had since first making sergeant.

CHAPTER 23

The Nail That Sticks Up

On Monday evening, Stanley called McGraw at work and asked if he'd handed out his leadership philosophy.

"Not yet," McGraw replied. "I was planning to do that today. I'm having some Mexican food brought in."

"That sounds good," Stanley said. "If you have any leftovers, feel free to drop them off at my house!" He laughed, then continued. "Seriously, I'm calling just to warn you: Don't expect too much of a reaction from your squad. Chances are good that none of them have ever seen anything like this before, and they certainly won't know all the effort behind it. So hand it out, let them know why you did it, offer to talk about it in private with each of them—if they want—and then settle down and enjoy your food."

The presentation of McGraw's personal leadership philosophy went almost exactly as Stanley had predicted. The squad members seemed a little puzzled when McGraw handed out the sheets. After giving everyone a few minutes to read through them, McGraw briefly explained why he had written his leadership philosophy, and how he had settled on several of the key points.

An awkward silence followed, and while McGraw was figuring out what to say next, Hardy blurted out, "Let's dig in!" That was all the signal the cops needed to go for the tacos and burritos.

McGraw went through the food line last, and found Hardy waiting for him at the end of the table.

"This is pretty great," he said, holding up his copy of McGraw's leadership philosophy.

"Really?" McGraw asked, a bit suspicious. "So you don't think I've written up my own death warrant?"

"Nah," Hardy replied, reaching into a bowl for a tortilla chip. "It's on them, now. If they're smart, they'll see what you've given them." He nodded toward the paper in his other hand. "This here is a treasure map. For each of them, these are the exact instructions for getting out of first watch in Sector Three forever."

McGraw chuckled. "I'm not sure they get that, or at least they haven't right away," he said. "Will you tell it to some of them?"

"You bet," Hardy replied with a nod. He turned and walked toward the tables where the rest of the squad was already seated.

As McGraw spooned salsa into his tacos, he saw Sgt. Jenkins enter the room, pick up a plastic plate, and plop a burrito onto it. Then Jenkins's attention was diverted by the extra copies of McGraw's personal leadership philosophy that were stacked on the edge of the table. He picked one up and looked it over. Then, when he was sure he'd caught McGraw's eye, Jenkins raised the sheet to his face and blew his nose into it, long and loud.

"Funny," McGraw commented without cracking a smile. "You're a million laughs."

Jenkins turned to walk away. "Here's my input," he giggled, waving the soggy paper. "I'll leave it in your box." Jenkins made his way to the row of cubbies against the wall that were designated for paperwork and shoved his erstwhile-handkerchief into the box marked "McGraw."

I'm not sure what else I expected from him, McGraw thought in disgust. Then, making an effort to put Jenkins out of his mind, he joined his squad to eat.

When the food had been reduced to crumbs, everyone started preparing for detail. McGraw was considering which items on his to-do list to tackle first when—*Oh no. Gus.*

"I need to talk to you, McGraw," Gus said by way of greeting. He picked up one of the sheets marked "Leader's Compass" and muttered, "What's this?" Ignoring McGraw, the lieutenant scanned the page and made a series of snickering noises through his nose as he went down the list.

"Okay, come with me." McGraw followed the other officer like a schoolboy and sat down across from his desk.

"I have written you up three times," Gus stated. He listed the incidents off on his fingers. "Failure to supervise your sleeping beauty Hitchcock, failure to provide proper training on the wagon crash, and failure to follow procedure on that domestic disturbance call with Hardy. I've also recommended that Internal Affairs investigate the domestic disturbance further." A nasty grin spread across Gus's face. "I have information that you may have had an inappropriate sexual relationship with the woman at that address."

McGraw was flabbergasted. "That's ridiculous, Gus!" he exclaimed. *How did anyone—Gus included—get such a crazy idea?*

"Ridiculous?" Gus suddenly raised his voice. "*This* is ridiculous." He held up McGraw's leadership philosophy. "You must think you're better than everyone else in this place. This leader philosophy b.s. and all your personal development claptrap? Forget it!" Gus balled up the leadership philosophy and slammed it into the trash can beside his desk. "You're not dancing your way between the raindrops on your way out of first watch in the substation. No, you're gettin' *soaked*, like everyone else around here. I'm seeing to that."

McGraw, who was fuming internally, said nothing.

"I'm going to file the failure to supervise on Hitchcock, because I want to prevent any chance of his coming back here," Gus continued. "The other two, I'm keeping in my drawer. I'm keeping the Internal Affairs recommendation in there, too. If you and that joker Hardy ever go over my head again, if I ever get sandbagged like that again, I will file these, and you will end up shuffling papers on administrative leave for the next two years." He glared at McGraw. "Any questions?"

"What are you saying, sir?" McGraw asked, unwilling to let the topic go. "Are you saying that we could have handled convention weekend without narcotics and vice helping us?"

"I'm saying don't *ever* leave me exposed like that," Gus growled. "I don't ever want to see units coming into my division without me having sent a request up the chain of command. Never." He stabbed his finger at McGraw. "Not if it's to save your own grandmother's life."

McGraw couldn't help venting his frustration. "So no good deed goes unpunished here?"

"You're damn right no good deed goes unpunished," Gus replied between clenched teeth. "Good deeds are for Boy Scouts, and the one thing I've learned about Boy Scouts in this department is this: They cannot be trusted. So the next time you try and do another one of your good deeds, just remember I've got your career here, right in this drawer."

McGraw gave a single, brief nod. "So that I'm clear, I still want to run my squad my way. Is that going to be okay with you?"

"Do what you want," Gus said, leaning back and shrugging. "Not that any of it will matter with the bunch of bums you've got. But watch your back with the other sergeants. They all think you're trying to show them up, and I'm not going to protect you from them." He smirked.

McGraw walked away from Gus's desk in a mild state of shock. He felt like calling Stanley, but instead, he picked up his leadership philosophy and started reading it to himself.

Hardy approached him from across the room. "Hey, what's up?" he asked. "What'd Gus say to you over there?"

"He told me he's written me up three times, along with an Internal Affairs complaint."

"Geez, really?" Hardy didn't try to hide his disbelief.

"He's still mad about Narcotics and Vice getting into the district last week," McGraw explained.

Hardy frowned. "Why didn't you just tell him I did it on my own?" he asked. "You could have saved yourself. We both know I'm on Gus's crap list anyway."

McGraw looked the other man in the eye. "It's not true," he said. "You told me you'd make some calls and I didn't try to stop you or ask you about them." Then he stopped and looked down at the floor. "Anyway, Gus said he actually filed only the 'failure to supervise.' He's hanging on to the others, including the Internal Affairs request, for now. That's what he said."

Hardy's face brightened. "He didn't even file the other complaints?" Then he laughed.

"I don't see the humor," McGraw muttered.

"Gus is a bigger coward than I thought," Hardy explained, still smiling. "If he really thought he could get rid of you, he would have put everything through the system. From what you just told me, I'd say he's more scared of you than you should be of him."

Makes sense, McGraw thought to himself. He could feel his negative mood beginning to lift. "Gus also told me to watch out, that the other sergeants might be out to get me."

"Sound advice," Hardy commented. The two fell silent for a moment. "You know, when I got knocked out of Narcotics, someone told me this old saying that 'The nail that sticks up gets hammered down.' That's you, McGraw. You're the nail that sticks up. Sometimes, you're going to get hammered."

McGraw thought about that. "I think it's worth it," he said. "Don't you?"

Hardy smiled. "I'm glad to hear you say that."

EPILOGUE

Validation

It was a half-hour before detail, and McGraw was cleaning up some paperwork on his desk when Hardy approached him with a stapled set of printouts in his hand.

"Take a look at this, Boss," Hardy said, then grinned. "It took six months, but you're famous."

McGraw scowled. Across the top of the front page was the logo of CopForum.org. It was a popular online bulletin board, famous for its nasty anonymous rants about the police department.

"I never look at this website," McGraw told the other officer.

"I know you don't," Hardy replied, thrusting the printout a little closer. "That's why I printed this out for you."

With a short sigh, McGraw took the papers and began reading them. The topic of the thread on the front page was "Sergeant's So-Called Leadership Philosophy," and the first posting was a tirade typical of the site.

"Six months ago, a rookie first-watch sergeant with too much time on his hands gave his squad one of the stupidest documents I've ever seen. He calls it his 'leadership philosophy' and it reads like a to-do list from Fantasyland. One item says 'I will tell the truth and I expect others to tell the truth.' Ha! Like anyone ever got ahead in this police department by expecting to be told the truth! The rest of this idiotic statement is even funnier. See for yourself!"

Pasted below the posting was McGraw's entire leadership philosophy. Seeing it reproduced and ridiculed in such a public forum made McGraw feel a little ill. He looked up at Hardy.

"Why did you give me this?" he asked, starting to feel angry. *I thought Hardy had moved past this kind of thing a long time ago.*

"Keep reading," Hardy urged.

A few short postings followed, generally making fun of the language in McGraw's prose. One post made a dumb joke about McGraw's community college education. After the fifth negative entry, though, the tide began to turn.

"I don't see the problem," wrote Donut12. "My sergeant is such a useless jackass, he'd never have the guts to put himself on the line like this. Give this sergeant some credit, whoever he is. It takes a stand-up guy to hand out something like this."

CharmingSam101 replied, "I agree. He doesn't sound like a bad dude to work for. I wonder what the reality is, though."

And then came the posting McGraw was not prepared for.

Galpatrol49 wrote, "I work for this sergeant and I can tell you that he has been the best thing to happen to me in three years in the dept. Before he came to our substation, I was so frustrated by the way my squad was run that I was ready to quit the force. Once he distributed this leadership philosophy, there was a big change in our shift. You can see the difference in our numbers. Crime in our sector is down 23 percent from last year. Arrests are up 7 percent, and response time is at a record low. We all have each other's back in our squad now because we are all working from the same playbook. We also know that our boss is accountable to EACH OF US, just as we are accountable to him and to the department. Can anyone else say the same about their patrol shift?"

"Galpatrol49?" McGraw murmured, his mind racing. Then the lightbulb came on. "This is Williams, isn't it?"

Hardy nodded his head. "Williams," he confirmed. "I've been working pretty close with her, but she never said a word about CopForum to me. She just wrote it up and posted it."

"She's made a lot of progress, hasn't she?" McGraw asked. Normally, he wouldn't say that the words "warm fuzzies" and "cop" went together, but he was certainly feeling them now.

"Absolutely," Hardy replied. "Very sharp. Very self-assured. And this tells you that she knows where it comes from."

McGraw paused for a moment. "I didn't want to tell you this," he finally said. "I didn't want to tell anyone here. But in the morning, after tonight's shift, I'm going over to Midtown

West for a meeting with some sergeants and lieutenants. They want me to talk about how to write a leadership philosophy."

Hardy's eyes widened. "Does Gus know?" he asked.

McGraw wasn't surprised that this had been the other officer's first thought. Gus had been strangely subdued for months. *Hardy probably doesn't want to see him get stirred up—neither do I, for that matter.*

"I think so," McGraw replied. "He hasn't said anything to me about it. But the invitation came to our chief from the chief at Midtown West."

Hardy breathed a sigh of relief. "For a second I thought you'd gone over Gus's head again," he admitted. "So you're just going to tell them about the process Stanley put you through?"

McGraw nodded and glanced back down at the printout in his hands. "I wish I could bring Stanley himself," he told Hardy. "He could explain it all much better than I can. But the chief said the meeting is for department members only."

"Stanley's a good guy," Hardy agreed. "But they want you. They want to know how you're making this work, in this department. Keep that in mind."

McGraw was honored by Hardy's assessment, but he still worried that he didn't have enough expertise to share with the group of sergeants and lieutenants. "I'm sure that's true," he began. "But they're going to have questions I might not have answers for. That's why I thought that Stanley should be there. He's coached lots of people through this process. He'd know what to say."

Hardy smiled. "Don't worry about it, Boss." He hoisted his gym bag over his shoulder and started moving toward the locker room. "You'll do fine. At worst, they'll hear you out and then do nothing. No shame in that. Being ignored is the usual reward for trying to help this department."

The shift that night was exceptionally quiet. There were a few calls on minor car crashes, some false burglary alarms, and the usual noise complaints after bar-closing. Radio calls had been down in the sector all month, and although McGraw couldn't be sure, he thought his squad was making an impact on street crime.

Months earlier, McGraw had decided to take Ramsey and Somers off patrol wagon duty for good, as soon as they had finished training their replacements. But instead of just throwing the two officers back into patrol, McGraw had given them an assignment. He had them work as a team to try to stop a rash of car break-ins just a few blocks off the Walnut and Grant strip. Ramsey and Somers had spent hours poring over the recent break-in reports, and they found a few telling patterns in time, place, and m.o. It took three weeks, but one night Ramsey and Somers arrested two young men, having surprised them just as they were breaking into a silver BMW parked in a back alley.

The two arrestees were arraigned and released on bail the next day. But Ramsey and Somers gave a printout of their mugshots to a grateful storeowner on the strip, and he distributed copies to all the other shopkeepers in the area. Some hung the pictures in their storefront windows. The break-ins stopped. The men had either found a new line of work, or had moved their operation to a different patrol sector. No one had seen them again in Sector Three since.

Reminding himself of these recent successes gave McGraw a much-needed dose of confidence as he made his way to Midtown West once the shift was over. The early morning sun was low and cast a long shadow in front of McGraw's car. As he merged onto the interstate, McGraw's phone rang. It was Stanley, returning his call. McGraw activated his car's built-in speakerphone system.

"I wanted to bring you with me today," McGraw explained. "But they said the meeting was department only."

Stanley was reassuring. "It's just as well," he said. "They don't want to hear old Navy stories, Adam. They want to hear you. They'll want to know about all the risks and rewards in running a patrol sector when the patrol officers have this document in hand. You can speak to that. I can't."

"I guess that will be enough," McGraw replied, trying to convince himself.

"Are your crime numbers still going in the right direction?" Stanley asked.

"Yup," McGraw said, reaching up to flip down his sunvisor. "So are the activity numbers. I think that's the main reason they called me in. Midtown East is the only division showing marked improvement, and it's mostly in my shift, my sector."

Stanley chuckled. "Everyone respects results," he observed. "Even in that police department of yours."

The Midtown West substation was on a tree-lined street just two blocks from the western edge of Central City's downtown business district. The building was the exact opposite of Midtown East's substation. Five years earlier, it had been thoroughly renovated, and the walls still looked as though they had been freshly painted. *Maybe they have been,* McGraw reflected. The front doors opened into a carpeted lobby where the main desk was located. The place felt cool, professional, and quiet. It didn't smell.

A sergeant led McGraw to a conference room where he met the chief and about a dozen lieutenants and sergeants, all seated around a large table. As McGraw was introduced to them one-by-one, he noticed that in front of each was a copy of his own leadership philosophy.

McGraw began his talk by describing how Stanley had introduced him to the idea of writing a leadership philosophy, and how, in the process, he'd learned for the first time what leadership really meant to him. He had begun to explain the connections he saw between issuing the leadership philosophy and the crime drop in his sector when he realized that no one was really listening.

They've been summoned to this meeting against their will, McGraw thought with dawning realization. *Crime is up and activity is down in Midtown West. I've been brought in as a form of punishment.*

He quickly wrapped up and asked for questions. Not surprisingly, there were none. The dozen or so sergeants and lieutenants stared at him blankly from around the table. Some had their arms folded in front of them and looked downright hostile.

"McCloskey!" the chief barked. "What would be your first concern about handing a similar document to your patrol officers?"

To McGraw's right, a man's head snapped up. Clearly, he had been taken by surprise. "Uh, well, I guess, Chief, I'd uh…I'd be concerned about having it stuffed in my face by a few of the troublemakers in the squad."

The chief swiveled in his chair. "What about that, McGraw?"

"I had that concern, too," McGraw began. "What I found, though, was that I was much harder on myself than any of my patrol officers could ever be. Once I'd put these commitments down on paper, I couldn't let myself get soft or sloppy with them." He glanced down at the document. "Especially the ones you see here about staying positive and energetic."

McGraw paused and thought about what he might say that would resonate with the other officers. "Some days, when everything's falling apart and it's one problem after another, I just feel like saying, 'I'm really teed off today. Go bother someone else.'" That got a few chuckles, so McGraw continued. "But I can't. Not when I've promised in black and white to stay positive and energetic. No one has to stuff that in my face. I know it because I wrote it."

A few more knowing smiles appeared around the table, and the tension eased.

"Did you get your lieutenant's approval before you wrote this?" the chief wanted to know.

"I didn't, and that was a mistake," McGraw admitted. "I've told him it was a mistake, too. I had to. Admitting my mistakes is right there in my leadership philosophy." The chief laughed.

"What about that?" asked one sergeant. He leaned forward with his elbows on the table. "How do you say, 'I was wrong' without it undermining your authority? If I'm your boss and I keep telling you how I was wrong, you might not want to carry out my next order, because you're thinking I might be wrong about that, too."

"I was concerned about that," McGraw replied. "But it doesn't work that way. These patrol officers are adults, and they like being treated like adults." Again, his words elicited several knowing looks. "I usually tell my squad I was wrong when it's already obvious that I was wrong. They know it whether I say it or not. But they appreciate hearing it. And that makes it easier for them to admit when they are wrong."

The room fell silent. McGraw wondered if he'd touched a sore spot. *Maybe the chief is one of those leaders famous for never admitting that he's wrong.*

"Any other questions?" the chief asked. A young female sergeant raised her hand. "These items here about 'no gossip, no whining.' If my patrol squad didn't gossip and whine, I think they'd be mute!" The whole room burst into laughter.

"There's still gossip and whining on my watch," McGraw told her. "It's just not as flagrant as it once was. People know to rein it in, because they've been notified that these are hot buttons for me. And you'll see that another one of my hot buttons is bringing up problems without proposing solutions. If I hear you whining or complaining, I might ask you what you intend to do about the problem. Whenever I do that, no one's surprised to hear it, because it's right there in my leadership philosophy. I want to hear solutions."

The chief began to wrap up. "Let's all thank Adam for coming out," he said. "We'll stay in touch and maybe someday soon I'll ask you to come back and coach the sergeants and lieutenants here on their leadership philosophies."

McGraw was puzzled. *Asking the sergeants and lieutenants to write a personal leadership philosophy seems a bit presumptuous if he's not going to write one himself.* Correctly interpreting the look on McGraw's face, the chief corrected himself. "And that includes me, too. I hope you'll be back to coach me on writing my leadership philosophy, too."

As McGraw rose from his seat, he felt there was one last thing he wanted to say. "You know," he began, "we're told to follow a lot of rules and regs in this department, and I think it's important not to confuse this document with just another set of rules. My friend Stanley compares it to a compass, a leader's compass. If you're lost in the woods, a compass will not get you out. It points the correct direction, which is valuable, but it's only a tool. You've still got to do all the hiking by yourself, no matter how tough the terrain."

On the drive back to Midtown East, McGraw wondered what would result from this meeting. He thought about the importance of setting an example as a leader. The chief at Midtown West seemed ready to assign his subordinates the task of writing leadership philosophies without creating one himself.

Maybe it was an oversight, McGraw thought. *Or maybe it's a sign of why, for all its sweet-smelling air and spotless walls, Midtown West has serious problems.*

Back at the Midtown East substation, McGraw gathered his belongings and checked his interdepartmental mail. He ripped open a letter from the commissioner's office, congratulating him on completing his six-month probationary period as a sergeant. The letter notified him that after completing one year, he would be eligible to take the lieutenant's test, which was coming up the following spring.

McGraw held the letter lightly in his hand, waving it slightly up and down as though he were weighing it. Six months earlier he'd felt completely unprepared for this job. Now, to his surprise, he found himself eagerly awaiting the opportunity to take his next step.

MY LEADERSHIP PHILOSOPHY

by

Sgt. Adam McGraw

I developed this philosophy to guide my actions as a leader, and I will strive to live and work according to these principles. I share it with my patrol officers so you will know the basis for my actions, and so you can let me know when I'm falling short of these goals.

My job as a leader is to influence people by providing purpose, direction, and motivation, while accomplishing the department's goals, improving the department, and supporting people as they try to reach their full potential.

People in organizations are happiest and work best when they have some control over their work and their careers, when they are engaged in meaningful work, and when they are treated with respect. I will be concerned with people and results.

I believe that people want to succeed. My job is to create an environment where that can happen.

I will tell the truth, and I expect others to tell the truth. This includes bringing me bad news when it's fresh, when we can still act on it. Bad news can still provide good data.

I will have the moral courage to make the tough calls. If I can't figure out what the right thing is on my own, I'll ask for help. When I do make a decision on a sensitive matter, I'll be willing to explain myself.

I will keep in mind that you have other obligations outside of work. To the extent that I can help make these aspects of your life fit together well, I will. In return, I expect you to work hard.

I will actively seek input and advice. Give me your honest counsel. If I don't think to ask, give it to me anyway.

If I see you do something or hear you've done something that may be ethically questionable, I will ask you about it. Don't be offended. When you see me do something you're unsure of, ask me and I'll explain myself. I won't be offended. We will be able to make ethical decisions together if we're willing to shine a light into those dark corners, if we're willing to challenge ourselves and each other.

I will keep my sense of humor, and so should you. I will maintain a positive outlook, especially in tough times, and will be energetic.

I will take responsibility for my actions and decisions, and so should you.

We all make mistakes. We will all try to learn from our mistakes.

When assigning duties, I will balance your need to try new things and learn new skills with the department's need for excellent results.

Accomplish your tasks on time. If you are going to be late, let me know just as soon as you figure it out.

Communication is the key to smooth operations and to building trust. We must make our concerns known and share feedback throughout the organization. We will be honest, and we will not indulge in personal attacks.

My hot buttons:

- If you lie to me or engage in misconduct, I will write you up.
- Be on time for detail.
- Don't gossip.
- Don't whine.
- Don't just point out problems. Propose solutions.
- Don't be afraid to make what I consider one of the bravest and most courageous statements anyone can make: "I was wrong, and you were right."

YOUR LEADER'S COMPASS

What is it?

If you've ever spent time wondering what your boss wants, then you know why a leadership philosophy is important. Just as a police organization's mission statement is designed to let police officers know what the organization is about, a personal leadership philosophy is designed to let police officers know what the police leader is about, what he or she wants, and what constitutes good—or bad—performance.

Your leadership philosophy explains the how and why behind your actions as a police leader. Writing it will help you clarify your own thinking. Publishing it will let your officers know where you're coming from. With a leadership philosophy, there will be less guesswork, less frustrating thrashing around as police officers try to figure out what the rules are, and less wasted time, money, and effort as plans are drawn and redrawn in the absence of clear guidance.

Publishing your leadership philosophy is an opportunity to spell out your commitment to consistent leadership. Good police leaders act consistently because they know what they believe in, are committed to those values, and act accordingly. Police leaders also understand that inconsistent behavior sends mixed signals, muddies goals, saps initiative, frustrates subordinates, sows distrust and even fear, and wastes everyone's time. When you are consistent, your officers will know what to expect. You build credibility with them and they feel they can trust you. This is why leadership style doesn't matter nearly as much as consistency. Police officers will adapt to many different styles of leadership, as long as their leader is consistent.

Writing a leadership philosophy is not an easy exercise. For one thing, in the busy work-a-day world, police leaders often have difficulty carving out some quiet, uninterrupted time to sit and think about leadership. There are always demands that seem more pressing, fires that need to be put out. You need to consider, however, that failure to think about leadership is like failing to plan. One doesn't need a great deal of experience as a police supervisor to know that having a plan, any plan, is far better than having no plan at all.

Second, writing a leadership philosophy means you will have to tangle with vague and sometimes difficult questions: "What do I believe in?" "What is important to me?" "Do I value people?" "What kind of leader am I?" "How do people perceive me now?" It takes courage and discipline to face questions like these. One of the main purposes of this book is to assure you that the effort is worth it.

Third, writing anything of substance is hard work. It requires patience and persistence, because hardly anyone gets it right the first time. Some of the best professional writers are those who accept that their first drafts are often really bad. They will tell you that all good writing involves *re*-writing.

Fourth, before you share this document with your officers, you will need to show a draft of your leadership philosophy to one or more persons close to you. As a reality check, you should share it with at least one person you trust and say, "This is how I see myself as a leader. Am I like this, or am I fooling myself?" You may not like what you hear, but if you are truly committed to leading effectively, you will listen.

Finally, distributing your leadership philosophy requires courage. When you share your philosophy with the whole police organization, it means that you are inviting people to hold you to all the promises made and implied in the document. Some leaders will be frightened by the possibility that they will be unable to live up to their stated goals.

It's important for you to understand that you will become a better police leader by making an honest effort to fulfill the promises in your leadership philosophy, not by attempting to be perfect. The goal of all this work is not to produce a clever, well-written document. You are taking these difficult steps because you have a genuine desire for improved understanding between yourself and your officers. Publishing your philosophy also demonstrates your sincere commitment to greater self-knowledge, self-confidence, and improved effectiveness as a police leader.

What should be in it?
There is no checklist approach for what should or shouldn't be in a leadership philosophy. Each is unique, because each is formed by a leader's own personal experiences and beliefs.

The best leadership philosophies, however, include the following:

Values: What I hold important (e.g., honesty, fairness, respect).

Ethics: Vital guidelines for proper behavior, based on my values.

Leadership principles: The behaviors I will engage in and would like to see others engage in (e.g., set the example, take personal responsibility).

Personal idiosyncrasies: My peculiar likes or dislikes (e.g., lateness, crude humor).

Your leadership philosophy should be written to achieve these four primary objectives:

- It offers insights about you, for the benefit of both you and your officers.
- It creates a framework to help ensure your consistency as a police leader.
- It contributes to a healthy organizational climate.
- If provides a touchstone of values you can turn to whenever you may feel lost, confused, or afraid.

How do I start?

Writing your leadership philosophy should be a journey of sorts that leads you to discover WHO you are, what you BE-

LIEVE, what you VALUE, what your PRIORITIES are, and what EXPECTATIONS you hold for yourself and others.

Here is the four-step technique used by Academy Leadership in its seminars, and described in the Adam McGraw story.

1. Define what you think an effective leader looks like.

Take a sheet of paper and divide it down the middle, from top to bottom. Write "BEST" at the top of one column and "WORST" at the top of the other. Think of the best leader you have ever worked for. List that person's defining characteristics in the appropriate column. What actions did the leader take that made a difference for you? What values did the leader express through those actions? What skills and abilities did the leader exhibit, both technical and interpersonal?

Then make a similar list on the other side of the page for the "WORST" leader you've encountered. What actions did this leader take that might have made you feel demotivated or confused? What values were expressed? What skills and abilities did the leader lack? Try to define each of these qualities individually. Avoid the temptation to simply write the opposite of what appears in the first column.

The point of this exercise is to help you figure out what "best" means to you, based on your personal experiences. Compare the columns. Are there similarities in the categories you chose? Does respect—or lack of respect—keep surfacing? Does it look like communication skills are important to your perspective on what makes a good leader? Write a short paragraph, just four or five sentences, that describes what makes a good leader and what makes a bad leader.

2. Examine your own leadership style and personality.

Use your best-and-worst list and your paragraph on good and bad leadership to exercise some self-analysis. Which of these characteristics do you currently display as a leader? How important are they to you? To others? Pick the top three or four behaviors and the values they represent. Try to put them in writing, as if you needed to explain them to someone else. What ethical rules can be drawn from these values? Write out these rules.

3. Write out the leadership principles you want to model and see in others.

Using the set of values and ethical rules you've just drafted, write down a series of principles that describe the type of leader you aspire to be. They may be in the form of "I will" or "I am" statements. Then write down a complementary set of values and rules you expect others to display under your leadership.

4. Make a list of your personal likes and dislikes.

By clarifying what your "hot button" issues are (e.g., "I will not tolerate lying."), you provide yourself and your subordinates with a clear understanding of what they can count on you for. Committing your "hot buttons" to paper is essential to being a consistent leader.

This first draft of your personal leadership philosophy should be no more than three pages. Set it aside for a week, then read it and revise it. Be clear and concise; if you can cut a word without changing the meaning, cut it. Substitute short, simple words wherever you see long words, jargon, or the latest law enforcement buzzwords. Repeat this process until you believe you have something that will help your officers understand what you want. The document will never be perfect, however, so you should resist your temptation to revise it endlessly.

What follows are the personal leadership philosophies of three law enforcement professionals, including that of Sgt. Roy E. Alston, coauthor of this book.

MY LEADERSHIP PHILOSOPHY

by

Sergeant Roy E. Alston, PhD
Central Patrol Division
Dallas Police Department

What Leadership Means to Me

Leadership is the ability to influence human behavior in order to accomplish organizational goals. The leader's task is to understand and carry out the organization's expectations and goals, while at the same time understanding people's needs and desires, their strengths and their weaknesses.

Personal Values

I personally value honesty, persistence, commitment, and motivation.

Honesty—I will always tell you the truth and I expect you to always tell me the truth. Telling a lie is of no value. As a matter of fact, lying always makes the situation worse. The wrath and distrust you generate by telling a lie is much worse than the lie itself.

Persistence—I will never give up on accomplishing our organizational goals and I expect you to never give up on our organizational goals.

Commitment—I will always do what I say I will do, barring some unforeseen and extreme circumstance. I expect you to always do what you say you are going to do, barring some unforeseen and extreme circumstance.

Motivation—I will always be motivated even when there are very good reasons not to be motivated. I expect you to be motivated even when there are very good reasons for you not to be motivated.

Operating Principles

I will never tell someone to do something I am not willing to do myself. I will always seek to have an informed opinion about the tasks my people are responsible for and I will be ready to step in to help them, working side by side. I will always ask for advice from those most experienced in a task or set of duties, but I want my people to understand that there will come times when decisions must be made. Not all of these decisions will be decisions that you favor. In that light, I want everyone to know that my decisions are made with the best interests of everyone in the organization in mind. I will never make a decision in a way that seeks to benefit me directly. Transparency is key to building trust, and trust is a fundamental leadership fuel.

Expectations

I see organizational goals as the bare minimum that is expected of all of us and I want you to see them the same way. I will always seek to accomplish the mission and will always seek feedback to make the process better. Understand that we can disagree, but once the time for talking is over and the time for accomplishing is at hand, we will move forward as a focused team. I will always share with the team whatever information I have that I am able to share. You will know what I know and I expect to know whatever it is that you know. I expect you to tell me how best to communicate with you, so that we remain on the same page, always.

Non-negotiables

- Everyone is clear on the values and mission of the organization.
- Everyone performs their duties by the values and mission of the organization.
- Disengagement and sabotage are not acceptable.

Personal Idiosyncrasies

- Do not let the work become your life. Have a life outside of work and most certainly have a passion that is not related to work.

- Be on time.
- Do not lie, cheat, or steal.
- Don't whine.
- Don't be the problem.
- Speak up.
- Admit when you have made a mistake, own the mistake, and move forward.

Feedback

Feedback is critical to our success. I welcome your feedback so that I can be a better leader. Feel free to approach me and give me feedback when you think I need feedback, regardless of whether the feedback is good or bad.

MY LEADERSHIP PHILOSOPHY

by

Deputy Chief Catrina Shead
Homeland Security and Tactical Intelligence Division
Dallas Police Department

This leadership philosophy is developed to guide my actions as a leader. My purpose is to provide clarity and transparency so that others may understand the position from which I lead. I strive to live and work according to these principles.

My responsibility and purpose as the Deputy Chief of the Homeland Security and Tactical Intelligence Division is to influence you by providing purpose, direction, and motivation, while accomplishing the division's mission.

My goal is to create an environment that consistently facilitates your success and the success of the division. Therefore, I will always be concerned with you and your results and our collective results.

To this end:

• I will always be honest with you and I will always expect you to be honest with me.

- I will always adhere to the policies and procedures of this department and this division, and I expect you to always adhere to the policies and procedures of this department and this division.
- I will always hold myself accountable for my actions and the performance of this unit, and I expect you to always be accountable for your actions and your performance.
- I will always inform you of any changes, updates, and issues, and I will always expect you to immediately inform me of any changes, updates, and issues you become aware of.
- I will always actively seek input and advice when problems arise, but will always make the final decision.
- I will always maintain high levels of integrity and ethical standards and will expect you to always maintain high levels of integrity and ethical standards.
- I will always be open-minded when mistakes occur and will make a decision on the outcome.
- I will always strive to learn from my mistakes and I expect you to always strive to learn from your mistakes.
- I will always expect all required documentation and procedures to be completed on time.

Personal Idiosyncrasies (those things I will not tolerate)

- Untruthfulness
- Theft

- Non-admittance of mistakes
- Tardiness
- Slow/no response
- Disrespect for your chain of command
- Verbalizing problems without seeking adequate solutions
- Crude humor

I look forward to continuing the great success this division has already built and to all that we are going to accomplish together.

MY LEADERSHIP PHILOSOPHY

by

Deputy Chief Vernon Hale
South Central Patrol Division
Dallas Police Department

The purpose of this document is to inform you of my philosophy on what I believe to be important in regards to leadership. I also want to provide some guidance on how best to interact with me with the understanding that I seek to best understand how to interact with you. In doing so, I hope you will come to understand why I do the things I do and learn to trust my actions and know where I'm heading.

First and foremost, I absolutely believe that any person, process, or product can be improved even if only by a small margin. My mission is to provide you with purpose, direction, and support, while accomplishing the goals of the city and the agency while also making each of us better at what we do.

My goals are to:

• Reduce both crime and fear of crime in our communities while ensuring you have the tools and backing you need to do your jobs.

- Create a good working environment by helping each of you move toward your personal and professional goals.
- Ensure we have the moral courage to distinguish between mistakes, missteps, and misconduct and take the appropriate actions.
- Create leaders at every level by actively seeking ideas and input from the experts (those of you doing the work).
- Ensure we all understand the decisions made by asking questions if we have them.
- Understand that we will not like or agree with every policy decision, but that we will do our best to learn it, teach it, and make it work, even while providing alternative solutions.

My expectations are:

- I expect every officer to be technically proficient at their jobs. Knowing what to do and how to do it is critical to the quality and service our citizens expect. Learning never stops. Every officer should seek out opportunities to continue their own personal education.
- I expect every officer to go about their business with honesty and integrity. These values should guide all of our actions and decisions.
- I expect every officer to take the initiative to get things done. Seek responsibility and be accountable for your results. I'd rather have people who take action, even if

they make a mistake. It is okay to make mistakes. We can learn from them.

- I expect every officer to maintain a healthy balance between work and home. Take care of your family, as they will be with you always. Balance between your physical, emotional, and intellectual needs. Don't neglect one at the expense of the others.

- I expect every officer to provide me feedback. Officers should feel free to talk to me about ideas that they may have to improve our unit or do things in a better, more creative way. Officers should feel free to tell me how I am doing as well. I believe in open communications. Do not tell me what you think I want to hear. Just be real and honest. But above all, keep it concise. Don't tell me in several paragraphs what you can tell me in one sentence.

What I will not tolerate:

- I will not tolerate differential treatment. Every officer and every citizen should be treated with respect and fairness. When we treat officers and citizens differently, for any reason, we erode the trust they place in the leadership of our organization.

- I will not tolerate a lack of procedural justice. There are many policies and procedures associated with professional policing. We should follow those policies and procedures as they are written so that no one can accuse us of being unfair or inconsistent.

- I will not tolerate officers who display a low work ethic or lack of initiative. The expectation is that we give 100 percent and then some as the situations require. There is no value in sitting on the sidelines waiting for situations to resolve themselves, or in someone else stepping in to take care of something that you can take care of right now.
- I will not tolerate whining with no viable solutions. I recognize we all have varying feelings and opinions about many things that take place within and outside of the department. Take the time to gather all the facts and formulate a solution to accompany your concerns.
- I will not tolerate excuses. I will be clear on my guidance and expectations regarding tasks and objectives at all times. If I am not being clear, ask for clarification before the task or objective is due so that I can help you accomplish the task or objective.

I am a human being with a family, hopes, and dreams, and I am prone to err. Try to remember that about me and I will do the same for you. I tolerate mistakes as long as they were made in an honest attempt to improve performance and do not result in damage to the self-esteem of citizens or other officers. With this document I commit to these values, I challenge you to ensure I stick to them, and I welcome your feedback.

ADDENDUM

More Thoughts on Leadership
Courtesy of Academy Leadership

Coauthor's Note:

Now that you have read the story of Sergeant Adam McGraw and his leadership journey, you may find yourself wanting to know more about leadership. You may find yourself wondering: What *is* leadership, really? Are there certain universal "rules" of leadership? What if my natural leadership style just isn't effective or inspiring? How can I find out where I am, right now, as a leader?

At Academy Leadership, we regularly work with clients who ask these questions and many, many others. In fact, we have created seminars and workshops to help answer them. (Sometimes, looking it up in the dictionary just isn't good enough!) It probably won't surprise you to learn that we have a wealth of materials prepared on the subject. Some materials are from our leadership curriculum. Others are questionnaires or worksheets. All are designed to help people think more clearly about leadership.

I've decided to include some important materials from our curriculum in addition to a self-evaluation questionnaire here. Perhaps they will help you jump-start the process of writing your own leader's compass.

If you would like to learn more about Academy Leadership and what we do, please contact us at 866-783-0630 or visit our Web site at www.academyleadership.com. Regardless, I hope you have enjoyed this book—and I hope the following materials will help you clarify your thoughts and beliefs on what it means to be a leader.

Dennis F. Haley
Founder and CEO
Academy Leadership

SELF-EVALUATION QUESTIONNAIRE
My Leader's Compass

Assess the status of your leadership philosophy and the extent to which others understand it. What do you really value? What are your priorities? How well have you shared these concepts with the people who report to your officers? How well have you shared these concepts with other officers in your chain of command? Read the following statements and indicate how often you exhibit the behavior by entering the appropriate number in the box. For example, if you never exhibit the indicated behavior, enter "1"; if you always behave as indicated, enter "4" and so on.

Options
1. Never   2. Infrequently   3. Frequently   4. Always

_____ 1. I often think about the values that are non-negotiable for me.

_____ 2. I have written the definitions of my non-negotiable values.

_____ 3. I live these values and often assess the consistency of my behavior with these values as a check on myself.

_____ 4. I have shared and discussed the meaning of my values and definitions with my officers.

_____ 5. My values are consistent with the department's values.

_____ 6. I support/enforce policies and procedures developed by the department because they are consistent with my values.

_____ 7. I clearly state my priorities to my officers.

_____ 8. I am confident that my officers believe that my values drive my behaviors and make me predictable and consistent.

_____ 9. I have stated clearly to my officers how I will evaluate their performance and potential.

_____ 10. I know that my officers have a clear understanding about which behaviors I will expect and those that I will not tolerate.

_____ 11. I have a well-developed leadership philosophy that I've widely disseminated to my officers.

_____ 12. I know that my officers fully understand my leadership philosophy because we've discussed it at length.

_____ 13. I have spent time with my officers helping them to develop their leadership philosophies.

_____ 14. I consult my officers when assessing my consistency with my leadership philosophy.

_____ 15. I take corrective action in changing my behavior when I discover that I have acted inconsistently with my leadership philosophy.

ANALYSIS

Determine your total score by adding all of your responses. Check your performance by reading the statements in the box below and then use the WIWDD chart to indicate actions that you will take to improve.

15 – 29:   You probably have not clarified for yourself what is important to you or for your work team. Your officers are probably "lost" and cannot look to you for guidance on what to do or how to act regarding leadership behaviors.

30 – 44:   You have obviously thought about what is important to you and act consistently with these ideas most, if not all, the time. You probably need to spend more time clarifying your core values and leadership principles and share/discuss with your officers.

45 – 60:   You have a well-developed leadership philosophy and have shared it as well as discussed it at length with your officers. Your behaviors are perceived to be consistent with your stated values and they are in line with the department's values. Encourage your officers to do the same.

What I Will Do Differently (WIWDD)

Regardless of how successful you've been at developing and communicating your personal leadership philosophy, there is always room for improvement. Identify the items indicating areas needing improvement and determine actions that you can take to improve. Indicate those behaviors in the WIWDD chart, below.

ITEM #	ACTIONS TO IMPROVE

Why Study Leadership?

"Leadership is not rank, privileges, titles, or money. It is responsibility."
— Peter F. Drucker

By definition, a leader is anyone who is directly responsible for taking care of people or for accomplishing goals through the actions of others. Leaders cause others to act by influencing their thinking, decision-making, and behaviors. Leadership is not a function of position; it is a function of role and activity. Organizations require confident leaders who have the character and competence to lead.

There are at least two major reasons why studying leadership is important. First, the role of an organizational leader is to achieve that organization's goals. Organizations either meet goals or fail to achieve them depending upon the effectiveness of their leaders. There is no substitute for effective leadership, nor is there any way to compensate for its absence.

The second reason for studying leadership is that leaders must strive to become the best they can be, because the people they lead deserve nothing less. An organization entrusts its leaders with its most precious resource: its people. It is the organization's people who do the work, no matter how difficult, no matter how boring, no matter how exhausting. In return, they should expect nothing less than competent leadership. Leaders owe it to those they lead to enable them to contribute meaningfully, to perform to the best of their ability, to know how they are performing, and to develop their full potential.

Leaders are entrusted with a great responsibility. They must embrace the organization's values and learn to apply specific leadership skills. Effective leaders understand and embrace the organizational ideology and have developed their own—their personal leadership philosophy—that is consistent with the organization's. Just as an organization's ideology is the unchanging foundation for an organization's culture and behavior, a personal leadership philosophy is an unchanging foundation for leader behavior.

Before developing a leadership philosophy, a leader must understand leadership itself—its definition, its principles, its various forms and styles and the relative appropriateness of these styles under differing circumstances. Likewise, one needs to understand one's self: one's own values, principles, personality characteristics, and style tendencies.

Leadership Defined

Because there are many different definitions of leadership, let's begin by articulating the one that we will use here:

Leadership is influencing people—by providing purpose, direction, and motivation—while operating to accomplish the goals and improving the organization.

Influencing people. This means getting people to do what you want them to do. There's more to influence than simply passing along orders. The example you set is just as important as the words you speak. And you set an example—good or bad—with every action you take and every word you utter, on or off the job. You must communicate purpose, direction, and motivation through your words and by example.

Providing purpose. Give people reasons to do things. Help them understand the larger purpose to their actions. This does not mean that you must explain every decision to the satisfaction of your people. It does mean you must let them know why they are being asked to do something and how they add value to the larger organization by taking action.

Providing direction. Communicate the way you want the task accomplished. Prioritize activities, assign responsibility for completing them (delegating when necessary), and make sure people understand the standards for quality and performance. In short, determine how to get the work done right with the available people, time, and other resources. Then communicate that information: "We'll do these things first. This group works here; that group works there." Know that people want direction, challenging tasks, training, and the resources necessary to perform well. Then they want to be left alone to do the job.

Providing motivation. Create conditions that give people the will to achieve, prompting them to take the initiative when they see a task that needs to be completed. Give people challenging goals if you want to motivate them. They did not join the organization to be bored. Get to know your people and their capabilities; give them as much responsibility as they can handle, then let them do the work without looking over their shoulders and nagging them. When they succeed, praise them. When they fall short, give them credit for what they have achieved, and coach them on how to do better next time.

Operating. Leaders act to influence others in order to accomplish short-term goals. Do this through planning and organizing, preparing (laying out the work and making the necessary arrangements), executing (doing the job), assessing (learning how to work smarter next time), and providing feedback on job accomplishment.

Improving. Leaders also focus on the long-term perspective. Although getting the job done is key, leaders must do far more than just accomplish the day's work. Strive to improve everything entrusted to you—people, facilities, and equipment. There will be new tasks and goals, of course, but part of finishing the old ones is improving the organization. People respect leaders who assess their own performance, identify mistakes and shortcomings, and commit to a better way of doing things in the future.

Leadership Principles

Some fundamental truths about leadership have stood the test of time. The following list, for example, was developed from a 1948 leadership study. These principles are as valid today as they were back then. Use them to assess your performance as a leader and to develop an action plan that improves your ability to lead:

1. Know yourself and seek self-improvement. Understand who you are, including your values, priorities, strengths, and weaknesses. Self-improvement is a process of sustaining your strengths and overcoming your weaknesses. It helps you grow professionally, increases your competence, and inspires the confidence of others in your leadership ability.

2. Achieve technical proficiency. Before you can lead effectively, you must have mastered the skills employed by the people you lead. You must train your people to do their own jobs while they understudy your job—so that they are prepared to replace you if necessary. Likewise, you must understudy your own leader, in the event that you must assume those duties.

3. Seek responsibility and take responsibility for your actions. When you see a problem that needs to be fixed or an issue that needs to be addressed, do not wait to be told to act. Organizational effectiveness depends upon leaders who exercise initiative, are resourceful, and take opportunities that will lead to goal accomplishment and organizational success. Encourage the people you lead to take the initiative within your stated intentions. When you make mistakes, accept just criticism and take corrective action. Do not avoid responsibility by placing the blame on someone else.

4. Set the example. People want and need you to be a role model. This is a heavy responsibility, but you have no other choice. If you expect courage, responsibility, initiative, competence, commitment, and integrity from your direct reports, you must demonstrate these qualities yourself. People will imitate your behavior—for better or for worse. Set high but attainable standards for performance and be willing to do whatever it is that you require of others. Share hardships with your people and accept that your personal example affects behavior more than any amount of instruction or any form of discipline.

5. Know your people and look out for their welfare. Commit time and effort to listen to and learn about your people. It is not enough to know their names and birthdays. You need to understand what motivates them and what is important to them. Showing genuine concern for your people builds trust and respect for you as a leader. Telling your people you care about them has no meaning unless they see you demonstrating it. If you fail to care for them on a daily basis, they will rightly assume that you will let them down when the going gets tough.

6. Keep your people informed. People do best when they know why they are doing something. Organizations succeed when individuals use their initiative in the absence of instructions. Keeping people informed helps them make decisions and execute plans within your intent. It encourages initiative, improves teamwork, and enhances morale.

7. Ensure that each task is understood, supervised, and accomplished. Your people must understand what you want done, to what standard, and by when. They need to know if you want a task accomplished in a specific way or how much leeway is allowed. Supervising lets you know if people understand your instructions; it shows your interest in them and in goal accomplishment. Strike a balance in how closely you supervise: Over-supervision causes resentment, but under-supervision breeds frustration. When people are learning new tasks, tell them what you want done and show them how to do it. Let them try. Observe their performance. Reward performance that exceeds expectations and correct performance that does not. Determine the cause of the poor performance and take appropriate action. This is accountability. When you hold people accountable for their performance, they realize they are responsible for accomplishing goals as individuals and as teams.

8. Develop a sense of responsibility among your people. When you delegate tasks, you show your trust in people and you encourage them to seek responsibility. Develop people's capabilities by giving them challenges and opportunities. People feel a sense of pride and responsibility when they successfully accomplish a new task. When you stretch them and offer them increased responsibilities as they demonstrate their readiness, their initiative will amaze you.

9. Train your people as a team. Ensure that individuals know their roles and responsibilities within a team framework. Train and cross-train people so that they are confident in the team's abilities. This will develop a team spirit among people and motivate them to perform willingly and confidently. Teamwork is becoming more and more crucial to achieving goals, but good teamwork is possible only under certain circumstances. People work well in teams when they have trust and respect for their leader, trust and respect for each other as competent professionals, and when they see the importance of their contributions to the organization.

10. Make sound and timely decisions. Do not delay or try to avoid a decision when one is necessary. Good decisions made at the right time are better than the best decisions made too late. Indecisive leaders create hesitancy, loss of confidence, and confusion. You need to know when to make decisions on your own, when to consult with others before deciding, and when to delegate the decision. Gather essential information before making decisions and announce decisions in time for people to react.

11. Employ your work unit in accordance with its capabilities.
Leaders must know their work unit's capabilities and limitations.
People gain satisfaction from performing tasks that are reasonable and challenging. They are frustrated if tasks are too easy, un-
realistic, or unattainable. If the task assigned is one that people
have not been trained to do, failure is very likely to result.

Role Expectations

Success of any organization depends upon individuals fulfilling their roles and responsibilities to achieve goals. Everyone, including leaders, has a role—a socially expected pattern of behavior that is usually determined by their status or position in the
organization. The degree to which leaders meet the expectations
of others and to which others meet the expectations of leaders
affects the organization's effectiveness.

Expectations of Leaders. Research indicates that people have
common expectations of their leaders. Ask yourself how others
would rate you on the following expectations:

- You offer honest, just, and fair treatment.
- You show consideration toward others as mature,
  professional workers.
- You give them the opportunity to work within a climate
  of trust and confidence.
- You show acceptance of errors and employ them as
  opportunities for learning experiences.

- You take a personal interest in others as individuals.
- You exhibit loyalty.
- You shield employees from harassment by higher-ups.
- You anticipate and meet the needs of others.
- You inform others of the purpose of their tasks.
- You provide clear-cut and positive decisions and instructions that are not constantly changing.
- You place demands on others that are commensurate with their capabilities—not too small and not too great.
- You give others public recognition for their good work.

Leaders' Expectations. Leaders likewise have common expectations of others. Assess how clearly you and other department leaders are communicating the following expectations:

- Officers fulfill their organizational roles as expected by their supervisors, managers, and leaders.
- Officers are responsible and exhibit initiative.
- Officers demonstrate loyalty through willing and obedient service to instructions, policies, and procedures whether in agreement or not.
- Officers display the moral courage to bring conflicts to the leader's attention at the proper place and time and in an appropriate manner.
- Officers deploy their full abilities for the good of the department.

- Officers take action even when complete information may not be available.

Leadership Styles

As a police leader, you must always be yourself. Any attempt to be anything else comes across as fake and insincere. Who you are determines the way you work with other people in fundamental ways. Some leaders can wade into a room full of strangers and within five minutes have everyone there thinking, *How have I lived so long without meeting this person?* Other very competent leaders are uncomfortable in social situations. Some people are optimistic and smiling all the time; others are pessimistic and sour. Most of us are somewhere in between.

Effective police leaders adjust their leadership styles and techniques to the experience of their people and the characteristics of their organizations. Being consistent and treating everyone fairly doesn't mean interacting with everyone as if they were clones of one another. In fact, treating everyone exactly the same is unfair, because different people need different things from their leaders. Some people respond best to coaxing, suggestions, or gentle prodding. Others need (and at times may even want) the occasional verbal equivalent of a kick in the pants. Effective police leaders are flexible enough to adjust their leadership style to each of the people they lead.

To determine the proper approach with an individual, a leader must take into account the full range of that individual's qualities and quirks—all the complex elements of human personality that make leadership so difficult and so rewarding. One of the many things that makes the police leader's job tough is that to get peak performance, leaders must determine what people need and what they're able to do—even when they don't know themselves.

Leadership style is not determined by what the leader thinks it is, but by how others perceive it. Leadership style can be described as the subordinates' perception of the leader's behavior pattern when he or she is attempting to influence, guide, or direct their activities. Therefore, a leader must be constantly aware of this perception and know how to best approach people in each given situation, in light of how that leader's actions are viewed by them.

When discussing leadership styles, many focus on the polar opposite extremes—the autocratic style and the democratic style. Autocratic leaders tell people what to do without explanation. Their message is, "I'm the boss. Do it because I said so." Democratic leaders use persuasion instead. There are several shades in between as shown on the following page:

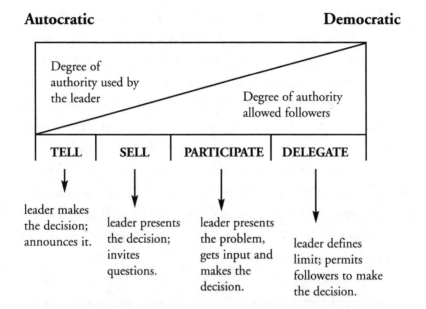

Autocratic   **Democratic**

Degree of authority used by the leader

Degree of authority allowed followers

| TELL | SELL | PARTICIPATE | DELEGATE |

leader makes the decision; announces it.

leader presents the decision; invites questions.

leader presents the problem, gets input and makes the decision.

leader defines limit; permits followers to make the decision.

Good police leaders vary their styles based on the situation, task, and people involved. There is nothing inconsistent about using different leadership styles in different situations. In fact, the very opposite is true. Applying only one leadership style to all tasks and situations indicates an inflexibility that ensures difficulties in areas where that style doesn't fit or make sense.

For the sake of discussion, the continuum between the authoritarian and democratic leadership styles can be divided into four basic categories: Telling, Selling, Participating, and Delegating.

Telling. This leadership style is characterized by one-way communication where the leader defines employee roles by telling them what to do, when to do it, how to do it, and where to do it. It is natural to expect a leader to use this style when dealing with a novice or during an emergency situation. In fact, people expect leaders to act forcefully and decisively during these situations. On the other hand, this style is likely inappropriate when dealing with an experienced and competent person, or when the task is complex and the leader lacks sufficient information. Using a telling style in such cases would show a lack of faith in an employee's abilities, and would risk making that person feel resentful and demotivated.

Selling. When a leader uses two-way communication to gain follower support by explaining and discussing the reasons behind decisions, the leader is using a selling style. Selling requires leaders to explain why decisions were made and then persuade the group to accept those decisions. It allows minimal participation by others, but it helps them to better understand and buy into the leader's decision. By taking people into their confidence, leaders gain support for their decisions and motivate employees to go along with them.

Participating. This approach involves leaders inviting their direct reports to be involved in the actual decision-making process. The leader using this style will typically discuss a range of possible alternative solutions with the group prior to making a decision. This requires good two-way communication and a willingness by the leader to be influenced by the knowledge and opinions of others. An example would be a shop foreman discussing with team members their estimates of completion times for certain stages of a project, and only then deciding on a course of action for sequencing the job.

Delegating. With this leadership style, a leader gives employees a mission to fulfill and allows them to accomplish it as they see fit. Essentially, the group is allowed to run its own show within the limits and guidelines established by the leader. The leader exercises minimal supervision, because the team has been provided with the necessary authority to complete the task.

Factors Influencing Leader Style

A leader should consider several questions when deciding upon the style that would be best in a given situation: Who is being led? What is the goal? What is the situation? Who am I as a leader?

Who is being led? Before determining the proper leadership style, the leader must assess individual and group abilities, experience, training, willingness, interest, motivation, group size and composition, and expectations. Obviously, experienced people should be led in a different manner from novices. The greater the ability people have to accomplish the task, the less direct supervision and guidance required from the leader. Motivation level will determine how much to push and how closely the leader needs to supervise to get the job done. The greater the willingness to accomplish the task, the less forceful the leader needs to be. Leaders must also know what their people expect, especially during transition periods between leaders. If you have a telling style of leadership, and you've recently replaced a leader who was a participator, you may experience difficulties. Your directions may be either misunderstood or ignored, because your style is out of step with what people had grown used to and now expect.

What is the goal? If a task requires a lot of coordination and attention to detail, leaders do not have much choice in style—they must tell how, who, what, and when it will be done. With simpler tasks, there is less need for specific direction from the leader and more opportunities for delegation.

What is the situation? The more time available to accomplish a task, the more opportunities there are for participatory and delegating leadership styles. For short-term, fast-moving situations, leaders need to tell and sell more often. In extreme emergencies and crises, leaders are expected to tell. They must take charge and make decisions. People look to their leaders on such occasions for direction. They expect concise orders, not questions and discussions.

Who am I as a leader? In general, the less confident you feel about yourself, the more likely you will have a telling, directive leadership style. Less confident leaders will usually go step-by-step until they feel they know everything is moving along properly. More mature, self-confident leaders, on the other hand, are inclined to be more comfortable with participatory and delegating styles. Personal values also affect a leader's natural tendencies. Those who tend to have more confidence in others are more likely to delegate and less likely to direct their employees on how to accomplish their tasks.

There are varying degrees of the basic styles based on the amount of authority the leader desires to use or delegate. A particular style of leadership might not be successful everywhere and might not be used effectively for everyone. What seems to be a telling style to one individual may be interpreted as a selling style to another. Sometimes people need to be told what to do because motivation, understanding, or experience is low; at other times, people need only a task statement to get them going.

ACADEMY LEADERSHIP SERVICES: DEVELOPING LEADERS YOUR PEOPLE WANT TO FOLLOW

In business, good management is about more than technical competency. To be truly successful, managers must also be leaders. That means having the ability to motivate and direct others toward achieving organizational goals. An effective leadership development program not only conveys those important lessons to participants but also shows them how to train their team members to do the same.

At Academy Leadership, we work with your organization to transform managers at all levels into effective leaders who can energize others to accomplish corporate objectives and create tangible business results.

Based on the leadership principles its founders learned at the Naval Academy and West Point—a passion to lead others, a persistence and drive to win, a focus on integrity, and the importance of clarifying each individual's contribution to the overall mission—Academy Leadership training, seminar, and keynote opportunities provide you and your staff with the essential skills you need to achieve business success.

Great leadership skills are at the pinnacle of what drives corporations to succeed. The best way to hardwire these leadership practices at your organization is through extensive and consistent training and leadership development. Read on to learn more about what Academy Leadership has to offer!

The Leadership Boot Camp Experience

An intensive three-day leadership skills training program led by former corporate executives and service academy graduates, the Leadership Boot Camp Experience is designed to transform your managers into leaders. This small-group seminar (limited to 15 people per session) shows your team how to improve business results by becoming better leaders. All who participate will come away more confident, more productive, more in-command, and better able to get things done through other people.

This is your team's chance to learn leadership *as it is taught at West Point and the Naval Academy* to the world's most successful military officers and future business leaders! The management and leadership skills taught at Leadership Boot Camp are based on military academy leadership principles and were developed and tested by an elite group of ex-military-officers-turned-entrepreneurs-and-CEOs. They have been battle-tested in the real world and are sure to generate real results for participants.

Send your organization's leaders to the Boot Camp and in return you'll receive men and women who are stronger leaders. They'll be transformed into effective managers who energize their teams, enable their people to see a clear relationship between their daily duties and organizational goals, communicate a consistent leadership philosophy throughout the organization, and instill smart work strategies in their team to achieve tangible results.

The Lead2Succeed Process™:
Creating Great Leaders and Sound Strategies from the Top Down

Most managers are technically competent but often lack the ability to motivate and direct others to achieve organizational goals. The Lead2Succeed Process helps solve this problem by converting managers into leaders who:

- Seek responsibility.
- Hold themselves accountable for their own actions.
- Train their people as a team.
- Make sound and timely decisions.
- Communicate effectively.
- Plan for success.
- Create a positive, enthusiastic, and supportive environment in which their team members can be successful.

There are four distinct components—Leadership Assessment, Focus & Alignment Workshop, Application and Action Sessions, and Evaluation and Follow-up:

- **Leadership Assessment:** Identify what types of activities energize great leaders and what activities energize or frustrate team members.
- **Focus & Alignment Workshop:** Determine the *purpose, values, vision, mission,* and *goals* that will guide your company into the future and provide the common thread for developing leaders.
- **Application and Action Sessions:** Take part in the training and application of selected leadership topics. These sessions help participants create a common "leadership language" and enable those at each level to coach and mentor others as they undergo the program.
- **Evaluation and Follow-up:** Learn to use periodic measurements and reports to determine the progress being achieved in individual skill development and the overall program goals.

Our program is designed to achieve results based on your company's specified goals. Lead2Succeed helps your organization achieve company goals, inspires employees to take initiative in indentifying and completing tasks, fosters better communication from the top down to the bottom up, and motivates employees to give their best every day.

The Vision-Based Strategic Planning Process

Where will your organization be in 10, 20, or 30 years—on the *Fortune* 500 list or out of business? To know if you are succeeding as an organization, you have to know where you are headed. This six-day intensive, interactive workshop helps you and your team create your company's vision and the strategic plan that will help you achieve it.

In addition to the preparation of the vision and strategic plan, we also work with you and your team to develop a systems view of your organization. This enables you to consider options for improving your organizational and management structures and improve your overall business focus and performance. And since changing your corporate culture is often a critical part of the plan, we also incorporate processes for accomplishing that in the workshop, and develop strategies to continue it.

Our proven Vision-Based Planning Process creates for you and your team:

- A vision that is truly shared by all your leadership.
- Clearly defined top-level goals by which to achieve your vision.
- Clearly defined, quantitative objectives by which to achieve the goals.
- Strategies by which to achieve each objective, including strategies for cultural change.
- Action steps by which to accomplish each strategy.

- Implementation plan.
- Metrics—MOEs and MOPs.
- Assigned roles and responsibilities.
- Stakeholder strategies for gaining and keeping their support.
- A War Room report providing the logic trail.

At the end of the planning process, you'll have a vision that is shared by all your leadership, clearly defined top-level goals, strategies for achieving them, a strong, cohesive team, and much more.

Lessons from the Battlefields:
Academy Leadership Experiences Explore the Past to Help You Create a Better Future

The Gettysburg Leadership Experience. An excellent opportunity to gain a deeper understanding of leadership, teamwork, and communication, the Gettysburg Leadership Experience brings senior executive teams to the site of the greatest battle ever fought in North America. Through on-the-ground study of the leadership challenges faced by the commanders in this pivotal battle of the American Civil War, participants learn practical, usable lessons that will benefit their organizations today and beyond. Participants gain new insights and new ideas on:

- How leaders can make the right calls amid murky, ill-defined conditions, incomplete information, and high pressure.
- The intricacies of decision making and communication in very large organizations, and how culture affects what's possible.
- How successful leaders share their vision for success, reduce the possibility of misinterpretation, and get everyone pulling in the same direction.
- How leaders develop imagination and courage in themselves and others.
- Why character, a central element of leadership, is the key to building trust on teams.

Our experienced team of leader-facilitators uses stories of key leadership moments to bring critical lessons to life in vivid detail. These lessons, in turn, render valuable insights into how successful leaders operate today.

Modeled on the U.S. Army Staff Ride, a technique used to train officers in leadership and decision making, the experience lets participants see and feel, as no history book or mere lecture can, the challenges commanders faced during these three pivotal days in our nation's history. Instructors provide the historical background and facilitate in-depth discussion to reach a deep understanding of "leadership in action." Executives leave excited about their opportunities to be better leaders and armed with battle-tested tools they can use immediately.

The Normandy Leadership Experience. Learn how to lead at the site of one of the world's great military operations—the 1944 Allied liberation of France. During the four-day program, you'll see and feel the challenges that were faced by commanders in WWII's pivotal battle. Instructors illustrate "leadership in action" by facilitating in-depth discussion on topics such as the strong character of Dwight Eisenhower and how it kept the allies working together, how exceptional leadership led to the victory of Pegasus Bridge, and how leaders kept their soldiers moving forward in the face of adversity on Omaha Beach. During this one-of-a-kind learning opportunity, you'll gain new insights and new ideas on how to:

- Build flexible organizations that carry on in the midst of chaos and rapid change.
- Develop leaders who are creative thinkers.
- Communicate strategic intent so that everyone understands and takes responsibility for the mission.
- Earn the trust of subordinates.
- Build strong coalitions, across cultures and generations, for competition in the global marketplace.
- Prepare the next generation of leaders.

Best of all, you'll leave the experience armed with battle-tested tools you can use immediately.

The American Revolution Leadership Experience: Concord Bridge. In the Concord Leadership Experience, executives visit the Minute Man National Historic site near Concord, Massachusetts, flashpoint of the American Revolution, to learn timeless lessons on leadership that can invigorate today's businesses. During a visit to the site of this 1775 day-long battle, participants learn practical, usable lessons about team building, morale and courage, dealing with ambiguity, effective communication, and the execution of strategic intent. These powerful tools will help leaders to energize their organizations and get them moving towards their business goals.

As with our other on-the-ground leadership experiences, walking this historic ground creates a learning atmosphere that is almost impossible to create in a conference room, because the experience, like leadership, is emotional as well as intellectual. Executives gain new insights and new ideas on:

- How leaders help the organization combat fear and uncertainty.
- The intricacies of contingency planning and war-gaming.
- How an organization's culture can be predictive of performance.
- How leaders influence morale.
- How leaders organize effective teams.

Participants leave ready to meet the challenges of leading in today's complicated business world head on.

Out of the Trenches:
Inspirational Leadership Messages to Help Improve
Your Organization

Are you looking for that perfect speaker or perfect subject for an annual company dinner, a professional association, or part of a larger event? The Academy Leadership staff has experience in speaking on a variety of leadership topics, such as leadership philosophy, productivity improvement, how to motivate people, how to manage conflict, how to develop future leaders, and more.

We can tailor a presentation to your audience and your specific needs. Whether you choose a keynote speech or one of our workshops, our programs will allow you to apply leadership principles to your organization's current situation. Your next company dinner could be the perfect opportunity to share valuable lessons in leadership with your staff.

Lead the Way Today!

If you would like to take part in one of Academy Leadership's results-driven workshops or training programs, or if you would like to book one of our speakers for your next company event, visit www.academyleadership.com or call us at 610-783-0630.

BOOKS FROM ACADEMY
LEADERSHIP PUBLISHING

The Leader's Compass for Law Enforcement Professionals: A Values-Based Approach to Influencing People, Accomplishing Goals, and Improving Your Organization
(2012, ISBN: 978-0-9727323-7-6, $24.95)
by Roy E. Alston, PhD, and Dennis F. Haley

The Accountability Compass: Moving from "The Blame Game" to Collaboration
(2012, ISBN: 978-0-9727323-9-0, $24.95)
by Dennis F. Haley

The Core Values Compass: Moving from Cynicism to a Core Values Culture
(2010, ISBN: 978-0-9727323-5-2, $24.95)
by Dennis F. Haley

The Corporate Compass: Providing Focus and Alignment to Stay the Course, 2nd Edition
(2009, ISBN: 978-0-9727323-6-9, $24.95)
by Ed Ruggero and Dennis F. Haley

My Father's Compass: Leadership Lessons for an Immigrant Son
(2006, ISBN: 978-0-9727323-4-5, $17.95)
by Perry J. Martini

The Leader's Compass: A Personal Leadership Philosophy Is Your Key to Success, 2nd Edition
(2005, ISBN: 978-0-9727323-1-4, $24.95)
by Ed Ruggero and Dennis F. Haley

Inspiring Leadership: Character and Ethics Matter
(2004, ISBN: 978-0-9727323-2-1, $24.95)
by R. Stewart Fisher and Perry J. Martini

Academy Leadership books are available at special quantity discounts to use as premiums and sales promotions, or for use in corporate training programs. For more information, please call Academy Leadership at 610-783-0630, visit www.academyleadership.com, or write to: 10120 Valley Forge Circle, King of Prussia, PA 19406.